STUDIES ON MODERN PAINTERS

Studies

ON

MODERN PAINTERS

BY

ARTHUR SYMONS

Essay Index Reprint Series

ND 190
S98

ESSAY INDEX

BOOKS FOR LIBRARIES PRESS, INC.

FREEPORT, NEW YORK

First Published 1925
Reprinted 1967

LIBRARY OF CONGRESS CATALOG NUMBER:

67-30233

PRINTED IN THE UNITED STATES OF AMERICA

CONTENTS

STUDIES ON MODERN PAINTERS: THE PAINTING OF THE NINETEENTH CENTURY

I

MODERN ART CRITICISM

THE modern criticism of painting in England has been for the most part somewhat accidental; we have had, since Ruskin, one or two good books and a number of good detached essays, but no body of really fine art criticism. The influence of Ruskin has undoubtedly been a good influence; beauty was to him, literally, as a Frenchman has called it, a religion; and he preached the religion of beauty at a period almost as much absorbed in the pedantries of science and the ignominies of material success as the present period. Much of his force came from his narrowness; you cannot be a prophet and a disinterested analyst at the same time. Ruskin did more than any man of our century to interest Englishmen in beautiful things, and it matters little whether his choice among beautiful things was always really the choice of an artist. He could convince the stubborn and Philistine British public, or he could brow-beat that public into fancying that it ought to be convinced. William Morris, who made all kinds of beautiful things himself, and who also tried to argue on behalf of beauty as a Socialist orator, has had very much less influence on the bulk of the British public. Morris, however, was really continuing the work which Ruskin began.

Had Walter Pater devoted himself exclusively to art criticism, there is no doubt that, in a sense, he would have been a great art critic. There are essays scattered throughout his work, the essay on *The School of Giorgione*, for instance, in which the essential principles of the art of painting are divined and interpreted with extraordinary subtlety. I remember hearing him say that, as he grew older, books interested him less and less, pictures delighted him more and more. But with him art criticism was but one function of a close, delicate, unceasing criticism of life; and the ideas at the root of painting, as well as of every other form of the activity of the spirit, meant more to him, in spite of his striving after absolute justice, than the painting itself. Thus, even in that admirable essay on Giorgione, he could leave out all mention of *The Geometricians* in the Vienna Gallery, as, in writing subtly about the ideas of Coleridge, he could leave out *Kubla Khan* from the selection of Coleridge's poetry which was to accompany his essay. As it was, he corrected many of the generous and hasty errors of Ruskin, and helped to bring back criticism to a wiser and more tolerant attitude toward the arts. .

Everything that Whistler has written about painting deserves to be taken seriously, and read with understanding. Written in French, and signed by Baudelaire, his truths, and paradoxes reflecting truths, would have been realised for what they are. Written in English, and obscurely supposed to conceal some dangerous form of humour, they are left for the most part unconsidered by the "serious" public of the annual picture galleries.

There is one book by another writer who has not always been fairly treated, George Moore's *Modern Painting*, which stands out among the art criticism of our time. It is full of injustice, brutality, and ignorance; but it is full also of the most generous justice, the most discriminating sympathy, and the genuine knowledge of the painter. It is hastily thought out, hastily written; but there, in those vivid, direct, unscrupulously logical pages, you will find some of the secrets of the art of painting, let out, so to speak, by an intelligence all sensation, which has soaked them up without knowing it.

II

THE LESSON OF MILLAIS

THE burial of Millais in St. Paul's should have been an honour done to a great painter, who died at the age of thirty-five, the painter of *The Eve of St. Agnes*, of *Ophelia*, of *The Vale of Rest*; it was but an honour done to a popular painter, the painter of *Bubbles*, and other coloured supplements to Christmas numbers, who died at the age of sixty-seven. In the eulogies that have been justly given to the former President of the Royal Academy, I have looked in vain for this sentence which should have had its place in them all: he did not make the "great refusal." Instead of this, I have seen only: he was English, and so fond of salmon-fishing.

It is not too much to say that Millais began his career

3

with a finer promise than any artist of his time. For sheer mastery of his brush he was greater even than Rossetti, greater than Holman Hunt, greater than Watts, greater than anyone but Whistler. He had the prodigal energy of genius, and painted pictures because he was born to paint pictures. It was at his studio that the Pre-Raphael-ite Brotherhood took form, and he was the most prominent member of the Pre-Raphaelite Brotherhood. He was elected an Associate of the Royal Academy at the age of twenty-four, a Royal Academician at the age of thirty-four. Up to then he painted masterpiece after masterpiece, pictures in which there was temperament, intuition, a noble interest. From that time to the time of his death he painted continuously, often brilliantly, whatever came before him, Gladstone or Cinderella, a bishop or a landscape. He painted them all with the same facility and the same lack of conviction; he painted whatever would bring him ready money and immediate fame; and he deliberately abandoned a career which, with labour, might have made him the greatest painter of his age, in order to become, with ease, the richest and the most popular.

Art, let it be remembered, must always be an Aristocracy; it has been so, from the days when Michelangelo dictated terms to Popes to the days when Rossetti cloistered his canvasses in contempt of the multitude and its prying unwisdom. The appeal of every great artist has been to the few; fame when it has come has come by a sort of divine accident, in which the mob has done no more than add the plaudits of its irrelevant labour to the select approval of the judges. Millais alone, since

4

the days of the first enthusiasm, in which he was a sort of fiery hand for the more slowly realising brains of his companions in art, has made the democratic appeal. He chose his subjects in deference to the opinion of the middle classes; he painted the portraits of those who could afford to pay a great price. His pictures of pretty women and pretty children had the success, not of the technical skill, which was always at his command, but of the obvious sentiment which makes them pretty. The merit of these interminable pictures varies; he was sometimes more careful, sometimes more careless. Mastery over the technicalities of painting he always possessed; but it had come to be the mastery of a hand which worked without emotion, without imagination, without intellectual passion, and without these qualities there can be no great art.

The newspapers, in their obituary notices, have assured us that in honouring Millais, we are honouring not merely the artist but the man: "of the Englishmen who have been the soul of Art," said *The Times* "scarcely one has deserved more than Millais." My thoughts have turned as I read these commendations of the good citizen, so English, so sporting, whose private virtues were so undoubtably British, to a painter, Simeon Solomon, also a man of genius, whose virtues were all given up to his art, and who was living (in 1896) in a destitute and unhonoured obscurity. It has seemed to me that there, in that immaculate devotion to art, I find the true morality of the artist; while in the respectability of Millais I see nothing to honour, for its observation of the letter I take to have been a desecration of the spirit.

5

III

SIMEON SOLOMON

ONE, the unluckiest, of those dreamers who have made a world *à rebours*, and have lived persistently in it "though the world," the other world, may have had only "a horror of their joy," is Simeon Solomon, a painter who lived on, forgotten, somewhere or other, until 1905, when his death in the workhouse opened to him once more the doors of the Royal Academy. It seems to me that he has his place, not far from Burne-Jones, in any record of the painting of the nineteenth century. Had circumstances been kinder to him, or had he been other than himself, he would have been a formidable rival for Burne-Jones, "where travellers of his tribe will still be waylaid, on the confines of glamour and sleep." Look through the catalogue of the Royal Academy and of the Dudley Gallery, between 1865 and 1872, and you will find picture after picture, from the *Lady in the Chinese Dress*, with its bad drawing and queer, orchid-like colour, and exotic and enigmatical expressiveness, to the Academy *Judith and her Attendant going to the Assyrian Camp*, of 1872. The very names, *Love in Winter*, *Sacramentum Amoris*, *Hosanna*, suggest Burne-Jones, though they are exactly parallel in date, and are as likely to represent an influence as a following. Others have a more definitely Jewish character, *The Three Holy Children in the Fiery Furnace*, the *Patriarch of the Eastern Church Pronouncing the Benediction of Peace*, the *Carrying the*

6

Law in the Synagogue of Geneva, while perhaps what was most significant in this strange temperament is seen in such pictures as *The Sleepers and the One that Waketh.* Three faces, faint with languor, two with closed eyes and the other with eyes wearily open, lean together, cheek on cheek, between white, sharp-edged stars in a background of dim sky. These faces, with their spectral pallor, the robes of faint purple tinged with violet, are full of morbid delicacy, like the painting of a perfume. Here, as always, there is weakness, insecurity, but also a very personal sense of beauty, which this only half-mastered technique is undoubtedly able to bring out upon the canvas, in at least a suggestion of everything that the painter meant.

In later years Solomon restricted himself to single heads drawn in coloured chalks, sometimes two heads facing one another, the Saviour and Mary Magdalen, the Virgin and the Angel of the Annunciation. The drawing becomes more and more nerveless, the expression loses delicacy and hardens into the caricature of an emotion, the faint suggestions of colour become more pronounced, more crudely assorted. In the latest drawings of all we see no more than the splintering wreck of a painter's technique. But as lately as ten years ago he could still produce, with an almost mechanical ease, sitting at a crowded table in a Clerkenwell newsroom, those drawings which we see reproduced by some cheap process of facsimile, in pink or in black, and sold in the picture-shops in Regent Street, Oxford Street, and Museum Street. They have legends under them out of the Bible, in Latin, or out of Dante, in Italian; or they have the names of the Seven Virtues, or of the Seven Deadly Sins; or are im-

7

ages of Sleep and Death and Twilight. "A void and wonderfully vague desire" fills all these hollow faces, as water fills the hollow pools of the sand; they have the sorrow of those who have no cause for sorrow except that they are as they are in a world not made after their pattern. The lips are sucked back and the chins thrust forward in a languor which becomes a mannerism like the long thin throats and heavy half-closed eyes and cheeks haggard with fever or exhaustion. The same face, varied a little in mood, scarcely in feature, serves for Christ and the two Marys, for Sleep and for Lust. The lips are scarcely roughened to indicate a man, the throats scarcely lengthened to indicate a woman. These faces are without sex; they have brooded among ghosts of passions till they have become the ghosts of themselves; the energy of virtue or of sin has gone out of them, and they hang in space, dry, rattling, the husks of desire.

IV

MONTICELLI

CLEARLY marked off from those painters to whom paint has been no more than a difficult, never really loved or accepted, medium for the translation of dreams or ideas into visible form, yet not without some of their desire of the impossible in paint, Monticelli seems to unite several of the tendencies of modern painting, in a contradiction all his own. I confess that he interests me more than many better painters. He tries to do a thing wholly his own, and is led into one

8

of those confusing and interesting attempts to make one form of art do the work of another form of art as well as its own, which are so characteristic of our century, and which appeal, with so much illegitimate charm, to most speculative minds.

To Monticelli colour is a mood; or is it that he is so much a painter that mood to him is colour? Faust and Margaret, or a woman feeding chickens, or a vase of flowers on a table, or a conversation in a park, or a cottage interior, it is as much the same to him as one title or another is the same to a musician. The mood of his own soul, or the fiery idea at the heart of these mere reds and greens and yellows: that is his aim, and the form which offers itself to embody that desire is a somewhat unimportant accident to him. But since form is the language in which alone we can express thought or emotion so as to be understood in any very positive or complete way, it is his error to be inattentive to language, forgetting how little we can express by gesture and the sound of the voice only.

But he himself, doubtless, is content with the arabesque of the intention, with a voluptuous delight in daring harmonies of colour, as a musician might be content to weave dissonances into fantastic progressions, in a kind of very conscious madness, a Sadism of sound. Monticelli's delights are all violent, and, in their really abstract intoxication of the eyes, can be indicated only in terms of lust and cruelty. Beauty, with him, is a kind of torture, as if sensuality were carried to the point of a rejoicing agony. His colour cries out with the pain of an ecstasy greater than it can bear. A weak and neurotic Turner, seeing fever-

ishly what Turner saw steadily in sky and sea, coupled
with a Watteau to whom courtly elegance and the delicate pathos of pleasure had come to be seen tragically,
sombrely, vehemently, might perhaps have painted some
of these pictures, or at least thought them in such a manner. The painting itself is like the way of seeing, hurried,
fierce, prodigal, the paint laid on by the palette-knife in
great lumps which stand out of the canvas. Looked at
close, some of these pictures seem to be encrusted with
uncut jewels, like the wall of the Wenzel Chapel in the
Cathedral of Prague. At the proper distance the colours
clash together in that irreconcilable way which Monticelli meant, crude tone against crude tone: their conflict
is the picture.

In writing of Monticelli it is impossible not to use terms
of hearing at least as often as terms of sight. All his painting tends towards the effect of music, with almost the
same endeavour to escape from the bondage of matter;
which happens, however, to be the painter's proper material, while it is not the musician's. Monticelli is scarcely
at all dependent on what he sees, or rather he sees what
he likes, and he always likes the same thing. He tries to
purify vision to the point of getting disembodied colour.
Other painters have tried to give us the spiritual aspect
of colour. He seems to paint listening. Confident, doubtless, in the symbolism by which a sound, a colour, or an
emotion may be identical, the expression only being different, not the thing expressed, he hears colour upon a
fiery orchestra of his own. And some of the formlessness
of his painting undoubtedly comes from that singular
confidence of his that the emotional expressiveness of

music, together with its apparent escape from formal reality, can be transferred without loss to the art of painting.

Does he not, however, forget that music is really the most formal and even fettered of the arts, a kind of divine mathematics, in which the figures on the slate begin to sing? At one end a dry science, at the other an inspired voice, music can express emotion only by its own severely practical method, and is no more the bird-like improvisation which it is often supposed to be than poetry is the instinctive speech of emotion when it has reached the stage of words. On true principles of analogy, music corresponds to a picture in which there is first of all very careful drawing. But that is not the way in which it is seen by theorists like Monticelli, whom we must take as he is: a painter who would make pictures sing, not according to the rules of music, but according to a seductive misinterpretation of them.

The subjects of Monticelli's pictures are excuses, and the excuse is sometimes almost humorous. He paints a woman feeding chickens, and the incident is only invented to bring a large figure, so over-real as to be almost spectral, against a background of blue-black storm-clouds. He paints a woman washing clothes, and, as one looks at the picture, one sees at first only a background crackling with flames, then a streak of white in the foreground, a river seen for a moment under the shadow of that great light, and then, finally, a woman bending over the water. He paints a nymph, and we see a coarse woman, half-naked, seated at the foot of a tree, with a dog at her feet. In another picture two dogs meet in a field, and stare curiously and angrily at one another. Sometimes he seizes upon a really picturesque moment, not neglecting its more obviously dramatic possibilities, as in the scene evoked from *Faust* or the sober and splendid Adoration of the Magi, in which the splendour of robes and crowns has not distracted him from the august meaning of the legend. He is fond of figures arrested in the pause of a dance, like the three Algerian women in the shadow of a doorway, or the tambourine dance in the open space of a park; curiously fond also of little naked children and of dogs. His painting often conveys the effect of tapestry, as in the large *Meeting in the Park*, with its colour as if stitched into the canvas. His world is a kind of queer, bright, sombre fairy-land of his own, where fantastic people sing and dance on the grass, and wander beside fountains, and lie under trees, always in happy landscapes which some fierce thought has turned tragic; the painter being indeed indifferent to more than the gesture of his puppets in solid paint, who make so little pretence to any individual life of their own. Their faces are for the most part indistinguishable; all the emotion being in the colour of their dresses, in their gesture, and in the moment's pattern which they make upon the green grass or against ancient walls.

And Monticelli has at least this great quality, among others less great: every touch of his brush expresses a personal vision, a way of feeling colour, and is a protest against that vague sort of seeing everything in general and feeling nothing at all, which is supposed to be seeing things as they really are. Things as they really are! that paradox for fools. For every one, probably, for the artist certainly, things are as one sees them; and if most people seem to see things in very much the same way, that is only another proof of the small amount of individuality in the average man, his deplorable faculty of imitation, his inability not only to think but to see for himself. Monticelli creates with his eyes, putting his own symbols frankly in the place of nature's: for that, perhaps, is what it means to see nature in a personal way.

V

CHARLES CONDER

CONDER was one of the rarest and most exquisite painters of our time; he could do what no other living man could do; he could be a wizard, and transform things into dreams and people into images. He can evoke all 1830 on the silken curve of a fan; he can paint what to other men is a verse of Verlaine, or the scent of a sachet, or a mood that never lost its fine essence in action. But he cannot give you the real face of a man or woman or thing; when he does not transform he is nothing; and you must give him the poet's license or be disappointed in your realist. He has tried to paint a portrait; and it is as if Verlaine had tried to write an epic. Let us think of *Il pleure dans mon cœur*, and of one of Conder's fans. Yet, always with Conder, one drifts into a rarer world than is lived in by lesser artists: a region of an almost morbid beauty where his fascinating creatures live exquisite lives.

He was our Watteau, a Watteau who has read Balzac

13

and been in Spain; he thinks about sentiment almost with the joyous sadness of the painter of *fêtes galantes*. There was no more authentic painter living, but he was uncertain, not only when he attempted work clearly not his own, like portrait-painting, but when he was doing his own work. In the fairy work of his fans, which are a little butterfly world of exquisite unreal sensations, where an eternal Mezzetin sings:—

> *Va! sans nul autre souci*
> *Que de conserver ta joie!*

the stain on the silk is everything, the flower-dust of the colours; and the uncertainty of the drawing counts for hardly more than a careless grace in the design. But when (as in such a drawing as the *Throne of the Peacock*, with its suggestion of Gustave Moreau, or in a lithograph like *The Spirit of May*) drawing is wanted, the lack of it is felt. It never need be felt in what must remain Conder's really individual work; in things like *Harlequin s'amuse*, or *The Leaning Tree*, where he is fragile, fleeting, 1830. But it is felt whenever he attempts the nude, because, like the French painters of the eighteenth century, he is the painter, not of the nude, but of the *décolleté*.

In an exhibition in 1905 at the Leicester Gallery I saw Conder's finest work; there, in his fans, his paintings on silk, and in his paintings on canvas, he showed himself as refined an artist on canvas as on silk. I do not say that even here the loveliest things are not among the paintings on silk: the *Balcony Fête in Seville* with its sense of multitude, the large decorative panel, the *Bullfight Fan*, *Under the Awning*. But there are pictures on canvas which can be named with these: a *Fête Champêtre*, a *Dance in Seville*, a *Mademoiselle de Maupin*, a *Gardener's Daughter* which has something of the quality of a Monticelli, and even a *Stormy Day at Brighton*, which is observed from nature, and with complete success. I said above that Conder is the painter of the *décolleté*, not of the nude; and in spite of the interesting quality of some of the nudes, interesting as colour, there is as yet no mastery of the human body as a whole, or only occasionally on the silk of a fan, where the flesh is not allowed to appeal to us as flesh.

Conder had no feeling for flesh as flesh, only for flesh as decoration; and this makes it the more surprising that ingenious persons in the papers have from time to time discovered I know not what signs of immorality in his work. He is a poet, and he paints. He paints lyrics; gesture in his pictures is like delicate sound, colour is itself an emotion. Not a line or tint comes there because, logically, it should come there; it comes as form and colour come into growing flowers. And, in his search for beauty, he seeks, like the Chimera in Flaubert, *des parfums nouveaux, des fleurs plus larges, des plaisirs inéprouvés;* and, through the intensity of his ecstasy of the senses, material things cease to be material, become spiritual. His naked bodies are the bodies of painted idols; they are perhaps "flowers of evil," but they are seen with a "vague and wonderfully void desire." Woman, to him, is seen always, seen like an obsession, but seen always through a dream. She is to him a part of all lovely colour, and he finds the loveliest part of her colour in the silken robes which she drapes about her, or half lets go, never wholly.

15

He sees her, not as woman the type (and thus not in the austerity of nakedness) but as the modern woman, whose appeal to us is always through the artifices of her toilette. Since Watteau no painter has had a subtler sense of the beauty and decoration of clothes, or has made rarer harmonies out of the modern opportunities of fancy dress. Spain has given him new feasts for the eyes, and has added new notes to the gamut of his colour: black and red, the colours of Spain, the colour of night and of blood.

I said that the rarest art is in creation of a new world. Conder has created a new world, with its sky, earth and people. His world is a park, with water and moonlight, in which a perpetual *fête galante* is in progress; or it is Triana, with the masquers passing in a car; or a silken ballet. He sees an exquisite, lanquid, voluptuous and musical delight, and with so complete an absorption in *l'heure exquise*, wherever that hour may strike, that there is never a false note in his harmony, a touch of affectation beyond the due measure of make-believe, as there is also no mere prettiness in all this strange and distinguished frivolity. No more sincere work has been done in our time; none which is more faithfully the expression of a temperament. Here is a man who has never looked frankly at any real thing, who has seen everything through a half-conscious veil of sentiment, who has chosen what he would see; but in whom choice has had the energy of an instinct.

NOTES ON THE GENIUS OF
AUGUSTUS JOHN

AUGUSTUS JOHN is, pictorially speaking, a man of substance: grave people say he is squandering his substance in riotous painting. The paintings, pastels, drawings, and etchings which he has lately been showing to a bewildered public in America and England, do not represent the whole of his resources; but, if you turn over a few portfolios of his drawings done in the tradition of Ingres, you will see work as precise and as punctilious and done with as much delicacy of skill as any by Ingres himself. Some of his etchings display a fine mastery in readings of character. They show a terribly direct eye, and a force of hand at least equal to the strength of sight. As yet, John has not enclosed himself within any formula; he ranges, a cheerful vagabond, across all the commons of painting; choosing here, rejecting there, and with equal strength to choose and reject. He is a great painter, and at present a painter in revolt.

John is not only a draughtsman, he is a satirist, and he is a purely pictorial satirist, totally unconcerned with ideas, setting paint and pastel to play games of their own, burlesquing Rubens and Rembrandt and Millet as only one great painter could burlesque another. He treats these painters and their subjects somewhat as Degas treated the manner of Ingres, bending the back of *La Source* over a japanned tub and setting the *Odalisque* to do side practice against an iron rail.

Take the pastel which has seemed to most people a

wanton desecration of the sentiment of Millet's *Angelus*. Millet would have praised it, for with Millet, sentiment was only part of a great sincerity, which in him was grave, noble, austere, because he saw the life of the peasant, not only frankly, but deeply. John's two uncouth animals, who embrace lumpishly in a field, are seen with all the superficial brutality of youth, but they are seen sincerely, and the energy of the handling makes them beautiful. John has never seen two English peasants in a potato-field standing in a reverent attitude; but he has seen them breaking out in amorous horse-play and he paints what he has seen.

Sometimes, as in his heads of gipsies, he paints monstrous wooden dolls instead of human faces; that is his way of being romantic. In one of his paintings, *The Legend of the Golden Mountain*, he is romantic to better purpose. There we see a violent reading of I know not what legend; a scene which bursts upon one, through flooding clouds, with all manner of explosive gesture, and solid apparitions. Energy sets it all a-start and a-gape; a thing which never existed exists for us now on the canvas.

His pastels are renderings of scenes and people who are still to be met with in English lanes and on the furze of English commons. Here is a camp of gipsies, the fire alight by the side of the *jivin vardo;* here is a humbler company of mummers; here are some poor actors, caught as they stand professionally by the roadside, disquietingly alive, shameless and joyous, jeering at themselves or at the spectator, in a very serious kind of foolery. In a few scrawls with the pen, indicating an attitude rather than a person, John brings life into a gesture, and sets a gesture talking with a singular vivacity. He amuses himself by taking nature always at a disadvantage; he waits on a woman's beauty until it sharpens or thickens into character; he waits on an abrupt gesture as other artists wait on a gesture which falls into some continuing curve. But what agility of truth in the noting of those movements! What power in the setting down of attitudes! And how colour, in these grasping, angry hands, becomes a weapon, a vengeance, a lyric!

There is not a picture of his which can please the buyer who buys for reminiscences of beauty. Every new artist, in whatever form of art, has to begin by destroying some accepted pattern which men have come gradually to recognize as beautiful. At present, perhaps, John is more busy in knocking down than in building up. That is an incident of growth and matters little. He has already shown his sensitiveness to beauty; you have only to disentangle the details of almost any of his pictures, which may offend you by its effrontery as a whole. And the effrontery itself, let us not misjudge even that. This resistance to the fashionable appeal of beauty *à la mode* is not deadness to beauty, but a fixed resolve to win some termagant gipsy enchantress, before whom the fine court ladies shall blush to their wrinkles. And meantime all the critics are warning John not to be ugly. "An ugly thing, I read in a responsible paper, "may be suggested in a sketch, and the suggestion may be pleasing. If it is realised too completely, its innate ugliness is apt to overwhelm the pleasure derived from the artist's skill."

What is ugliness in a picture? Manet's pictures used

19

to be called ugly; a woman in a tub, drawn by Degas, used to be called ugly, because the woman was naked, and not "nude." Goya would certainly be called ugly if he were not Spanish—and dead. Every well-bred lady still thinks Daumier ugly. Ugliness, I am inclined to think, is the name given to life which has not yet been apprehended. To the ordinary observer, as to the ordinary painter, only certain things in nature are beautiful; we admire the Arab horse and not the English donkey; the field of corn, and not the field which is alive only with weeds; the young girl of fifteen, and not the aged beggar who sings a lamentable tune as she hobbles along by the curb. But we have only to look closely enough and we shall realize that life is never ugly. Beauty or ugliness is in our own eyes, and not on the object on which we look. If John is ever ugly, it is not because he has represented women with irregular features and shapeless clothes, the weeds instead of the flowers, but because he has drawn them without love of life, without respect for life, without trust in life.

Perhaps sometimes he has. But he is young, and he has a natural desire to avoid highroads, and to take any short cut that will seem to lead him on his way, through whatever gaps in the hedge. He is in a very wholesome revolt against the academic principle in art, and I think he can be trusted to find his own way, because he is not in revolt against what he cannot do.

John's most daring simplifications of drawing conceal no lack of knowledge; he omits nothing that he could not fill up as easily as he can do without it. At present all his faults are faults of excess. He is a little too conscious of what the public likes, and a little too resolved to do something else. It does not matter what the public likes, or what other painters have done. Only life matters, and the sight of one's own eyes. John insists upon seeing so frankly that he sees—not only the wall—but *through* the wall. Was ever anyone so much more real than life? And, while he realises so keenly that art, in Mérimée's phrase, is *exaggeration à propos*, he has not yet found out for himself where what is *à propos* ends, and what is unlimited begins.

If Rossetti had been living he would have said of John's pictures that they were "stunners." No other word can give a quite adequate idea of the forthright achievement, the vital draughtsmanship, the splendid modelling, the abounding life, of such heads as the two studies from the same model called *Ardour* and *Dorelia*, the head of an old man, and the drawing of *Goton*. Is this last meant to be a study for one of the least decorous heroines of the Memoirs of Casanova? There is a Goton there, certainly unforgettable, who may perhaps have sat, in John's unhesitating head, for this brilliant drawing. But the name, however characteristic, means little enough in such painter's work as this, snatched straight from nature. Its appeal is direct and final.

John is already, I suppose, known to everyone who cares for such matters as a great draughtsman; he here shows himself, and for the first time, as one who is capable of becoming a great painter. The pictures of his which I have seen till now were obviously experimental, and none of them quite fulfilled the promise of the drawings. But in the three paintings I have named, and in the half-length portrait called *Carlotta*, which one would imagine to have led up to them, not without a slight hesitation by the way, there is mastery, and in the heads, an intensity of characterisation which goes further than any of the rapid summaries of the drawings, and seems to be wrung out of the features by an act of violence. In the set grimace of *Dorelia* and in the gaily diabolical wildness of the eyes and cheeks in the *Ardour* there is something which gives grandeur to vulgarity. They are set there with a kind of angry indifference, which is part of the humour of young strength; and they cry out against the dolls of all the studios. There is in them nothing but sound work, work done with a wise simplicity and economy of means; there is absolutely no display, nothing that calls off the attention from a single downright aim; they may be said to imply a hatred of the pretty and the ordinary, but do not more than imply it; there is, certainly, only a hand firmly and copiously at work in obedience to a firm and copious will to see.

The chief interest of exhibitions is certainly the affirmation of the talent of John, because John is a new man; but there are two or three other pictures which come only next to his in their arresting power. In Sargent's acceptance of material, of anything to try his hand on, there is none of the conviction which seems to clench itself with an oath in the pictures of John. But how his two canvasses live! In the *Sketch* a jaunty and insolent person, dressed with ostentatious inattention, setting his heels hard on the floor, and facing close scrutiny with his hat crushed defiantly upon his head, not only jumps as the phrase is, out of the canvas, but seems to jump literally in it. Part of its aim is to startle, and it startles; part, to give you without selection, a handful of life, and life moves to you, as your eye receives it. The *Studio* is a small picture very cunningly composed, an aspect caught on the cross with a luck which is no doubt mere skill. The man, the character of his attitude, the angle of the small room, with the bed, the sprawling sheets, the coloured sketches tossed hither and thither, the tilt of the canvas across the bed, the picture still wet on the canvas: all this is rendered with a direct, accidental art which lassoes things seen and drags them violently whither it will. And it has not only skill but beauty, a sense of what is actually beautiful in casual things seen anywhere, under the natural magic of light. It is a momentary escape into liberty and the private lust of the eyes, of the painter of imperial portraits.

After these pictures, which all assert themselves, and force you to stop before them, there is a picture that draws you towards it by a different kind of attraction. Rothenstein's *Deserted Quarry* is the finest picture he has yet painted, and deserves the praise that was given to his *Talmud School* of last year, when he was but feeling his way towards this more definitely achieved result. Here, at last, he has rendered, in his careful and deliberate way, an aspect which has given up its beauty to him, reluctantly but almost completely. The design is curiously original, and there is a brooding quality, an emotion made directly out of this great angle of black beams against the upper rocks and the sky, the shapes of the rocks, precise and yet mysterious, the dark rich colours retreating uneasily into the shadow from the lighted foreground; there is a bare and solemn poetry in it, as of a crabbed and coloured lyric of Donne. Only the technique still remains not wholly in keeping with the conception; as in the picture of last year, but not so painfully, there is a gloss which does not quite allow that conception to achieve itself in any real capture of the texture of natural things.

It is here, in precisely this capture, and often in so little beyond it, that Steer's strength lies. His *Storm* is by far the finest of the three pictures which he exhibits, and, in the fierce sky and suddenly revealed foreground, in the lonely and resistant tree standing like a tower on the edge of the thunder-cloud, there is a sense of awe, a rendering of the temperament, and not only the texture of a landscape, which is remarkable in his work. The water-colour drawing of *Hardshaw Scar* has scarcely less force in its grip of an aspect. But the *Twilight*, a landscape against a warm sky which is reminiscent of more things than nature, is, while being a capably painted picture, no more than the equivalent of what in literature would be second-rate poetry; it reveals no individuality, is no new reading of nature, as the *Storm* in its own way certainly is. The *Portrait in Black* loses by being set but a frame's length from John's half-length of *Carlotta*. There is a marvel of a gilt cane chair, a lovely curtain, a black dress painted as cleverly as the black domino of last year; and beyond, nothing. Now a portrait, even if it be no more than the study of a model, and part of a study of light and texture, should be, first of all, a portrait; especially when the head is treated, as it is here, at least as minutely as any part of the properties. Yet this head is inane, not because the model may have had an inane face, but because Steer has copied her face as if he were copying a chair, and with less sympathy for the meaning of her eyes and mouth than for the actual pattern of the chair upon which she sits. Turn from this study of a woman to the study of a woman by John which hangs beside it, and notice, in not the most startling of John's paintings of life, how much more there is in this look, gesture, attitude, in the whole person sitting there; notice how freely she breathes, and how the other sits and holds her breath to be looked at.

Having made himself a great draughtsman with the pencil, John has not yet made himself an equally great draughtsman with the brush, and his paint as paint is not nearly equal to his drawing as drawing. What suavity he has of it he has thrown away on a design which he mischievously calls *Cupid and Nymphs*, in which some swollen women lounge uncomfortably in a meadow. One realises that he has seen Rubens, and has caught from Rubens anything you like but the essential thing; that glory of flesh which puts a spirit of life, divine in its way, in every overgrown body that wallows, or reels, or collapses in every canvas of his. Here we get not the frank animal, but a gross and unilluminated satire on the animal. So, in the *Mother and Child*, which is splendid in its telling of character, powerful in modelling, and legitimately daring in at least the intention of its colour, there is something not only disconcerting, which would not matter, but meant to disconcert, which does matter; a sort of injustice to the thing which the painter can do, and is so nearly doing, with complete vigour. The grip of character

25

and form, the grasp of an aspect, is unflinching, nothing else in the room so much as competes with it. But the paint is less certain, does its work with less exactitude; and the final pleasure which we get from this painted picture is undoubtedly less great, less satisfying, than the pleasure which we should get from the same group if John had drawn it in black and white. The beauty of the drawing is obscured by the indifference of the painter to paint. In another picture, *Flora*, in which there is more aim at a kind of elegance, there is even less success; because elegance is snatched at violently, and partly missed, while the angry energy of the other picture is left out, as no part of the plan.

In Steer's piece of figure-painting which he calls *Morning* we shall find an interesting contrast to everything which we have noticed in John's work, except a certain rough vigour of handling, which both have in common. Steer is a landscape painter, and his landscape here is fine, arresting, done with as much feeling as the hand can give when it is not the agent of imagination, it is strong, capable work, showing us an aspect of nature with undeniable assurance: arresting, as I said, not captivating. But this genuine landscape painter, when he paints men and women among their furniture, confesses in their vacant faces and empty gestures how little he sees in them except as targets for light. The sofa on which his model yawns is delicious; its texture is there, visible and tangible: but the model turns a face of uncomprehended humanity to the morning. The pattern of the same doll was seen and painted before this by Albert Moore; she was more like marble then, but she has not yet come to have a soul. John's models may care little about having a soul either; but it is there, like an inquisitive child prying through a keyhole, looking out, defiantly alive, under threatening eyebrows.

There are three pictures and two drawings by Orpen which are among the cleverest things in the exhibition. How is it that, in spite of their cleverness, their outer sincerity, they leave us uninterested? There is a nude painted with extraordinary fidelity, a woman who sprawls on a bed; and her flesh is painted so that you might take it for real flesh; and yet there is no illusion, she remains unvitalised, academic. The work is painstaking and able, it follows truth for its own sake, yet offers truth a sort of platonic homage, not wrestling with and overcoming truth. John is not cleverer in the hand than Orpen, but look at the one beside the other! Here, indeed, John is not to be seen at his best; but take the little sketch called *In the Tent*, and see how much significance there is in its for once quiet statement of things. There you see a man painting to please himself, and though Orpen may very likely also paint to please himself, the result is work which can only please the public. His representation of actual things, so careful and effective, goes no further than the observation of a practised eye can direct the working of a skilful hand. With John there is a faithfulness to something more than the form of things, to the life and essential spirit of form. Look at his drawings and look across at Orpen's. It is Bohemia against Bloomsbury, sharp elbows and pointed shoulder-blades and rags against the finest baby-linen and the sleepiest fatness; but the children whom John has set down as if he hated them have come to life under his pencil and the children whom

Orpen has set down gently and cautiously will never wake up out of their sleep.

When we can say of a man's work that it is alive, what may we not hope for in it? Being alive, it has only to grow. Growth, it must be remembered, is not merely a blind force of nature, but owes its strength and direction partly to care and forethought. Will this remarkable draughtsman turn into a great painter? He has it in his own hands, but strong hands are spendthrift, and John seems at present anxious rather to scatter than to build.

There is as much vigour of a certain kind in Steer as in John, and a far greater mastery of paint. But why is it that John paints a sullen woman in a gipsy tent and makes you want to have the picture always on your walls, while Steer paints a school-girl with a far more complete kind of pictorial success and leaves you indifferent to her? The English school-girl has presented Steer with a subject absolutely "made to his hand," and within the limits which that subject set to his intelligence, he has succeeded perfectly. It is indeed the first time that he has painted a face with as much apparent interest as he takes in a dress or in furniture. One sees a masterly capacity to do a given thing, and the thing is done. Why would we rather have John's suggestion than Steer's assertion?

Again, Steer has a landscape which is technically by far the finest landscape in the room. It is a fine, solid, brilliant piece of work, with a serious sky and with water that is an almost deceptive image of water. It stands there and challenges denial, and it is not to be denied. Yet it is without greatness, it is without something which is the root of greatness. Look across from it to a small

28

and too rashly coloured landscape by John, a moor with a gipsy van, and you will see in it something which is not in Steer's landscape. That something I would define in a phrase of Browning: "The moment eternal." John snatches the eternal moment and throws it away; but Steer's average moment will never become eternal.

FANTIN-LATOUR AND
WHISTLER

IT has been said by a penetrating and suggestive
French critic, Charles Morice, that the course of
Fantin-Latour, in his work, may be traced "from the
real world to the dream-world through a garden."
He began, it is true, in the sixties, with studies from life and
lithographs from mythology, both together; but in the
main, the "realistic work" (the portraits and the flower-
pieces) was done earlier than the studies from music and
from dreams. In the pictures now on view at the Obach
Gallery we see work of each period, very fairly represent-
ative, and we see by a glance at the exquisite *Portrait of
the Artist's Sister*, painted in 1861, that whatever quality of really pictorial imagination can be distinguished
in the late, more professedly "ideal" work, is already
implicit, and we may think in a more satisfying measure, in the earliest, when the artist has not yet grown
tired of the visible world.

Everyone who has ever entered the Luxembourg will
remember the picture which represents Manet painting
in his studio, with Zola and a group of friends standing
around him. How good it is, how trustworthy, how search-
ing in its study of all these types of the artist; but, at
the same time, how chilling to the eyes. It is not a thing
caught just thus, but a collection of people painted one
by one, and set there very intelligibly before us. Fantin
never saw the visible world as it was, even in these early
portraits after nature, or in the early studies of still-life.
He loves flowers, but individual flowers plucked and put in

glasses, not a landscape, which scarcely occurs in his work; definite objects, like the white cup and saucer (No. 8), which he makes into a beautiful thing, all by itself; carefully chosen faces, mostly those of one kind or another of artist, each very carefully individualised, as in that *Coin de Table*, which has preserved for us the face of the young Rimbaud. It is not a way of seeing reality, but a way of picking certain choice things, a flower, a fruit, a face, out of reality, and reproducing just that, just as it is. Finally, and as a natural consequence of this selection (to which he adds copies of great pictures, which are like interpretations) he can find nothing any longer in reality that contents him, and he takes refuge in dreams, among wild lights and supernatural gleams, among phantoms of poets and musicians, Wagner, Berlioz, Byron, Schumann; himself most like Schumann, a cloudy dreamer, to whom Astarte comes on a cadence that is like moonlight. He has always sought rarity, and now he seeks ecstasy, which he would fain transpose from other arts into his own art; he would find short cuts to ecstasy, being a little tired of all there is to pore over and copy in the single flower, the single face. The lithographs snatch a filled cup too hastily and part of the music is spilled.

Among Fantin's paintings at the Obach Gallery there are a few, like Nos. 19 and 21 and 23, in which an imaginative conception, finely mysterious, is rendered with a certain dull glow of colour, really, in the true sense, lyrical. In No. 38, *La Danse*, where the veiled shapes are brought out into sudden light, it is as if morning had come upon a dream. There is no longer beauty to divine, but something very like prettiness to see; and in such late pictures as the *Aurora* and the *Venus and Cupid*, something waxy and almost like a trail of Bouguereau comes between the painter and his vision. In the lithographs, which are mostly dedicated to music, an attempt to render the essence of, for instance, the Prelude to *Lohengrin* in a design, there is invention, always in a sense pictorial, but rarely, I think, on a level, as pictorial invention, with the music which it sets itself to interpret. Looking at that particular design, I see a very ingenious translation from sound into visible outline; it is intelligible at once, one approves it critically, as a conception, but one cannot abandon oneself to what it says with these shapes, upward motions and scattered lights, as one can to the vast and exquisite ebb and flow of the tidal music. The lithographs are all romantic, in a Byronic or 1830 sense, a little operatic even; and they cannot take themselves lightly, as decoration, or mere whim; they are almost German in their emotional seriousness, or, as in *Le Poète et la Muse*, out-rhetoric French rhetoric.

To go from the company of the Fantin-Latours to the company of the Whistlers at the New Gallery is to pass suddenly from a world never quite real into a world as real as day and night. It is a world in which I, for one, find almost everything that I have ever cared to see, or to linger over, in what we call the real world. Here, at least, I see through a painter's vision the world which I have always lived in, a world which is full of beautiful appearances, and which, with all its fulness and satisfaction, is only a shadow and symbol of some supreme beauty, which we can see only through that shadow, but which is assuredly enough for one life. It is Whistler's reality that astonishes me the most, and the variety with which he represents that reality, going clear through outward things to their essence, that is, to their essential reality; never, like Fantin, setting up an invention in the place of nature. It is remarkable that an artist who may seem, in his words, to have denied nature, or to have put himself arrogantly in the place of nature, should, in his pictures have given us no image, no outline, no shade or colour, which is not evoked out of a thing really seen and delicately remembered. Tracing the course of these pictures from first to last one sees the technique changing from what is in a sense a realistic to what seems an evasive manner; from the Courbet-like *Wave* of 1861 with its shouldering strength and heavy paint to the *Nocturne, Blue and Green* of the Thames water asleep, or to those aspects of people and things in which a butterfly seems to have left a little of its coloured dust on a flower as it alights and passes.

Each comes closer than the last to something really seen, but with a vision more and more subtle and stealthy. He begins by building his world after nature's, with supports as solid and as visible. Gradually he knocks away support after support, expecting the structure to support itself by its own consciousness, so to speak, at the perfect moment he gives to the eye just enough to catch in the outlines of things that it may be able to complete them by that imaginative sympathy which is part of the seeing of works of art. But he can never be content with that service, and demands ever more and more of it in his challenge with things, with himself. And he comes finally to suppose that, after all, our eyes have the sight and

33

sensitiveness of his own; which is as if one were to expect the A B C class to read Euclid off the blackboard. The attitude towards Whistler of the older critics and of the public of yesterday was that of a rather vulgar curiosity. He had shown them a glimpse, and they wanted a gulp; and they pressed close to the canvas to see what a policeman sees when he turns his bull's eye on the lock of a door. But the closer they got the less they saw, and they went away in a rage and said there was nothing to see. A great man did a great wrong by doing that: the picture which he thought a pot of paint flung in the face of the public is in the exhibition to-day, exquisite in its beauty; and what Ruskin could do seemed to receive a sanction for the public which had just got far enough to see Ruskin. The other picture, which Burne-Jones bore witness against, is there too, the *Nocturne in Blue and Silver* (No. 12) and I had been sitting in front of it for a long time, drinking in its cool and remote harmony with unusual delight, before someone came up to me and told me that it was this picture which seemed to Burne-Jones (who yet had a sense of humour) like a bad joke. Vulgar curiosity is never gratified in any of Whistler's pictures. He never stared at nature, and you must not stare at his pictures. He treated nature as a gentleman treats a lady, and his fine manners were rewarded by exquisite revelations. I am sure that when he was painting a portrait he tried not to see his sitter, but to let that sitter surprise him, as a delicate artist in words lets himself be surprised by ideas, each surprise being like a sudden light. There is always a certain stealth about magic, and the magical quality did not come into Whistler's pictures by a forth-

34

right effort. But he prepared for it, and with ceremony, as one prepares for the reception of a guest.

In this exhibition of Whistler's work there are nearly a hundred paintings in oil, with a smaller number of drawings in water-colours and pastel and black and white, more than two hundred lithographs, and almost five hundred and fifty etchings. Into such a world, so variously beautiful, one cannot enter rashly or walk there hastily. To attempt to realise it at once in detail would be like trying to crowd sixty moments of separate ecstasy into a single hour. I have tried to set down one or two general impressions, or to sum up those impressions a little; I must leave it till I am able to come closer to the individual picture.

A SECOND VIEW OF
WHISTLER

IT is a rare accident which has allowed us to see the most complete exhibition which has yet been made of Whistler's pictures within a week of the closing of the most complete exhibition which has yet been made of the pictures of Watts. Each has his own world. Watts paints always with a sense of the glory of the world, of human glory, of the supreme glory of the spirit, or of God, which maketh all these lesser glories. No detail stops his vision, or puts out his hand, which sweeps freely, at home among splendours. His is a kind of heroic work, in which there is only nobility and affluence; every colour and every contour is noble and ample, only sometimes the painter's enthusiasm for things loses the subtler beauties which are in them, and so loses truth, as well as this more intimate beauty, by this way. He paints, certainly, the world he lives in; and what more can anyone ask of any painter?

Whistler, too, has his own world, which is neither splendid nor affluent, but an exquisite and exact world of shapes and shades, evoked with certainty and aloofness, the artist's aloofness from the aspects which he chooses for his own pleasure, out of visible things. And, in his disinterested greediness, which would follow and capture the whole of his own part of the work, he experiments with many mediums, and has many manners, though only one style. Each of his pictures has its "minutely appropriate" beauty, its "minutely appropriate" handling. In *The Blue Wave* we see him literally working with

Courbet and this, like the Breton seascape, and the building of Westminster Bridge, has the direct, almost violent truthfulness of Courbet. In *At the Piano* we have all that was most significant in the Pre-Raphaelite movement summed up; the *Shipping in the Thames* with the pale greys and pinks, the ghost of a landscape, is pure Puvis deChavannes; in *The Purple Cap* we get all Albert Moore, and how much besides! Whatever *The White Girl* owed to Rossetti was a debt already paid before the picture was finished. Japan and Velasquez, whenever they are seen, are seen through creative eyes. And just as in the landscapes and seascapes we see the paint thinning, clarifying, becoming more and more exquisitely and exactly expressive, so in the portraits and figure pieces we can trace the elimination of effort, the spiritualising of paint itself; in the white, for instance—cold in the *White Girl* of 1862, more luminous in the third *Symphony in White* of 1867, and finally, in the *Miss Alexander* of the early seventies, a white which is like the soul of a colour, caught and fixed there by some incalculable but precisely calculated magic. It ends, of course, by being the ghost of a colour, as in *The Convalescents*, but all things in Whistler end, when their particular life is over, by becoming the ghosts of themselves. All Whistler's portraits are at once disquietingly real, and at the same time, perfect pieces of decoration, in which the pattern loses nothing because it is made out of a living thing. And no two of the portraits are alike, but each is surrounded by precisely his or her individual atmosphere; each lives with a reality which is unlike the reality of any other. It is enough to look from the portrait of Carlyle to the portrait of Sar-

37

asate, and from that to the portrait of Duret. Does not Carlyle live grimly, and as if angrily silent in the empty room? And Sarasate, poised airily as if he heard the music of the violin in his hands before he drew the bow across it, emerging out of darkness? And Duret, a solid figure, correct, mundane, with the pink domino held like a bibelot? Each is an evocation, and each interprets, while seeming to exist only for the lines or colours of an Artist's fancy. It was part of Whistler's wise method to declare his indifference, as a painter, to what might be thought the "meaning," in literary terms of anything that he painted, but has he not said also that in portrait painting it is for the artist "to put on canvas something more than the face the model wears for that one day; to paint the man, in short, as well as his features?" It is the aim of Whistler, as of so much modern art, to be taken at a hint, divined at a gesture, or telepathy. Mallarmé, suppressing syntax and punctuation, the essential link of things, sometimes fails in his incantation, and brings before us things homeless and unattached in middle air. Verlaine subtilises words in a song to a mere breathing of music. And so in Whistler there are problems to be guessed, as well as things to be seen. But that is because these exceptional, difficult movements of nature, these twilight aspects, the re-glimpses in which one sees hardly more than a colour, no shape at all, or shapes covered by mist or night, or confused by sunlight, have come to seem to him the only aspect worth caring about. Without "strangeness in its proportion" he can no longer see beauty, but it is the rarity of beauty, always, that he seeks, never a strange thing for the sake of strangeness;

so that there is no eccentricity, as there is no display, in his just and reticent records. If he paints artificial light, it is to add a new, strange beauty to natural objects, as night and changing lights really add to them; and he finds astonishing beauties in the fireworks at Cremorne Gardens, in the rockets that fall into the blue water under Battersea Bridge. They are things beautiful in themselves, or made beautiful by the companionship and co-operation of the night; in a picture they can certainly be as beautiful as stars and sunsets. A picture is finished, said Whistler, "when all trace of the means used to bring about the end has disappeared." No one so rarely failed to know when that moment had come; but in two studies of a model on a couch, of which one is called a completed, and the other an incompleted print, it is the uncompleted which is the finer, and every added touch of colour a cheapening of the magic. It was part of the taste raised to genius in Whistler that he almost invariably knew when to stop. Look at a tiny, indistinct sketch in water-colour on tinted paper (No.169 in the North Room). It is nothing and it is enough, for it is a moment of faint colour, as satisfying in itself as one of those moments of faint colour which we see come and go in the sky after sunset. All the little water-colours at the entrance of the South Room (from 39 to 43) and more beyond, are among the things that no one but Whistler has ever been able to do in painting; Verlaine has done the equivalent thing in poetry. They have their brief coloured life like butterflies, and with the same momentary perfection. No one had ever cared to preserve just these aspects, as no one before Verlaine had ever cared to sing certain bird notes.

Each was satisfied when he had achieved the particular, delicate beauty at which he had aimed; neither cared or needed to go on, add the foot-note to the text, enclose the commentary within the frame, as most poets and painters are considerate enough to do.

In the etchings and in the lithographs we see, on opposite walls of one room, two worlds, each a peopled world of its own: the world of the etchings more precise, as of a real world seen, however choicely, in terms of literal reality; the other, a more vaporous world, in which things and people are seen with softer outlines, in an atmosphere more wholly that of twilight. It is rare in either to come across anything that can be said to have a subject, like the early etching of *The Miser*. The subject was in the aspect, and Whistler finds it just as well and as adequately for his purpose in the *Lobster Pots* of No. 174, or in the *Savoy Scaffolding* of 217. The real secret of Whistler, I think, is this: that he does not try to catch the accident when an aspect becomes effective, but the instant when it becomes characteristically beautiful. Take his miraculous lithograph of Mallarmé, that slight sketch, as it seems, for which he had forty sittings, and which looks as if it had been done in half an hour. Manet's portrait used to hang by the side of Whistler's at Mallarmé's but even Manet, who could do so many things that Whistler could not do, had not caught the poet of the *Faun* at that precise moment in which Whistler had caught him, and in which he had revealed the course and significance of a life time. Manet is without strangeness, he sees with tenacity under the absolute guidance of light; but with Whistler it is hit or miss, a nervous trial of skill which, like the acrobats, must succeed almost every time, as if his life also were staked upon it.

ON THE PURCHASE OF A
WHISTLER FOR
LONDON

THE Triumph of Whistler has been one of the great and conspicuous triumphs in our time of genius over prejudice, of genuine and original genius over false conventional art. The painters and the art critics, and the official persons and the man in the street were against Whistler from the first; he flourished his painting in their faces as the banderillero flourishes his red cloak in the face of the bull. It is the death of the bull, one of the recurrent and propitiatory deaths of the eternal and sacrificed bull, that we celebrate in the purchase for the nation on the part of the National Art Collections Fund of a picture of Whistler which was once derided in a British law-court with Ruskin and Burne-Jones, each an honest man of genius, bearing false witness against it.

Whistler, of course, delayed his public triumph by his impatience for it. He had not the strength to be patient, sit still and wait. He thought he "did well to be angry," because he saw himself in the light of a martyr for principles or of the imprisoned Galileo. His little poisoned arrows, that rankled but did not kill, kept up a guerilla warfare really on behalf of justice, though they might seem to be shot from under cover of wounded vanity. It is idle to say that they did not do havoc among the enemies, though they kept the fighter too long under the flag of a bandit.

Whistler by his writing did for art in England something like what Poe did for literature in America. Those criticisms of the *Literati*, which we read to-day with such a sense of labour wasted, helped to scour New York of scum, but they kept Poe back from recognition as the one great impersonal artist whom America has produced. His anger was a scourge for fools, and the fools cast back mud. Some of the mud stuck, and seemed to discredit him in the eyes of the fine gentlemen of the moment. It seems even now, as if we must forgive something to the artist because he condescended to be a fighter. Just as Whistler made it a little difficult for persons of limited comprehension to abandon themselves to the charm and magic of his canvasses because they saw in front of them a nimble duellist, whom they called Jimmy, keeping his paint-brush in the air "like a dancer."

Whistler kept back his own triumph, but the national forces of things may be trusted to keep back the recognition of any new truth or beauty which comes into the world. Blake said, in one of the wisest of his scraps of divine doggerel:

> *Some people admire the work of a fool,*
> *For it's sure to keep your judgment cool;*
> *It does not reproach you with want of wit;*
> *It is not like a lawyer serving a writ!*

Truth and beauty come upon the unprepared and the indifferent "like a lawyer serving a writ." They come to accuse and to awaken the world, not to gratify the world in its sleep. Is it not tragic that the better must always be the enemy of the good, and that the fittest should survive by the destruction of what was once fittest? Youth and beauty are hungry harpies, toothed and clawed, parricides and matricides, or, if they do not kill their parents, they thrust them out of doors, helpless with age.

The painting of Whistler came at a time when the public was beginning to accustom itself to the minute religion of the eyes which the Pre-Raphaelites had brought in; and the public, though it may have many loves contemporaneously, can have but one creed at a time. Ruskin by much preaching had brought the public to its knees; it was not convinced that it liked Pre-Raphaelite pictures, but it was certain that its duty to its higher self condemned it to accept them as what it ought to like. Imagine a poor public convinced that the manner of "The Awakened Conscience" was the manner of all great art, and then brought face to face with this particular *Battersea Bridge*, which seemed to it a wavering blue ghost, a trick of moonshine, the imposition of a juggler! There are still people who are so little able to use their eyes that they cannot see the absolute "truth to nature" of that picture; and how many painters since that time, besides Whistler, have been training the natural timidity of the eyes, leading it to see more than it had ever believed, and to believe in the long run, whatever it could see. Here was a choice of subject, a way of painting, which had no relation with those devout details of the older school; and if the one was religion, the other, certainly, must be heresy. So said the public, and so, alas! said Ruskin. And so Whistler had to wait for the new eyes of the new generation; and he had to train the sight of those eyes, to accustom them to take in new images of familiar objects; so every great original painter has had to do in every generation.

44

Of course, nothing is ever new, neither what we see nor how we see it; it is only that things have been combined in a new way or seen from new angles. If Whistler had really broken with the great traditions of art, if he had been original to the degree his admirers or his detractors (which with least reason?) are often found asserting, he would have been no more than the charlatan that Ruskin no doubt took him to be. A friend of mine told me that the chief impression made on him by the Whistler exhibition at the New Gallery was how imitative Whistler had been. On all those walls one saw Whistler, Whistler learning, and the most beautiful picture there, the most exquisite and the most masterly piece of painting, the portrait of Miss Alexander, cannot be thought of apart from Velasquez, though indeed with no limitation of its proper originality. What Whistler learned he put to his own uses, and he refused to learn anything which would serve none of his purposes. Well, the world in general has come now, by whatever means, to accept this particular man of genius at something like his real value, and there will probably be no voices so out of date as to re-echo any of the old cries against him, marring the general welcome of the picture which has been bought for London. But I see in the "Athenæum" the brilliantly ironical suggestion that now is the moment for the guardian of the Chantrey Fund ("The least they can do at this date to show their good faith") to "complete the representation of Whistler at the National Gallery of British Art by adding to the Chantrey collection a fine example of Whistler's portraiture." The moment, surely, would be ill chosen; for would it not be a confession of defeat?

The Chantrey authorities have hitherto been nearly consistent in their rejection of genius, their patronage of
mediocrity. They have successfully withstood the temp-
tation of every new force, even after the general public,
after long resistance, has at length succumbed. They represent to-day the only perfectly immovable conserva-
tives, the only impregnably entrenched forces of inaction.
To admit a Whistler, even in the comparative safety of
death, into their midst, would be to admit the very principle of disintegration. They would no longer be official
persons representing official views; they would have capit-
ulated already to the taste of the best judges, reinforced
by the loud, ignorant, and at last prevailing plaudits of
the mob.

WHISTLER AT THE CARFAX GALLERY

THERE is an exhibition at the Carfax Gallery, and you are asked merely to see "some oil paintings by deceased masters." I like the vague prose of the invitation, and I like to see Whistler and Blake together, Goya and Richard Wilson, the school of Antwerp and the school of Siena. It is a relief to pass from one to another among no more than thirty-four pictures of such widely differing styles and periods. A few broad contrasts or comparisons may indeed strike one, but one is not teased into trying to weigh the merit of this with that picture, painted at the same time and with a similar intention. Bonifazio pleases me the more after I have looked at an early Turner, and from the *Dutch Babies* I pass with fresh curiosity to the strange faces of *Lord Rochester's Children*, the shy girl and sanctimonious boy. And there is a Blake which calls to one, among so many pictures painted with so much more of the craftsman's skill. Christ heals the blind man, a Christ reverently heightened, like a human pillar; and the blind man is full of wonder and ardour as he staggers vehemently and uncertainly forward, and behind him is one of Blake's old men, like Samuel covered with a mantle, and coming up out of the grave; and all the background is of hills, stained with mysterious light and sombre colours. But the picture which one sees first and returns to last, in this choice and varied collection, is the picture which hangs at the end of the room, Whistler's portrait of Connie Gilchrist, dancing with a skipping rope. That picture was one of the portraits most conspicuously missing from the Whistler Exhibition. Even after the portrait of his mother, of Carlyle, of Miss Alexander, it needs to be seen, if one is to realise every corner of Whistler's genius as a portrait painter. It is different from any and like the others, it is the creation of a pose. He reveals to us a little, exquisite, pathetic creature, caught in a moment of harmonious movement, as the feet touch the floor between two turns of the skipping-rope. It has passed, it is coming again, it turns in the air, and the thin childish body is arrested as if literally in the air; a ghost of form in a ghost of movement.

In Whistler's portraits the pose itself is as much a part of the interpretation as the painting; and the quality of a portrait such as the Sarasate is not to be judged, as it commonly is, by the apparent lack of seriousness in it. Boldini's startling portrait of Whistler himself was an example of the art which tries for this common kind of success; there was the likeness, and the shining hat, and as much real artistic sense as is contained in a flash-light. Even in Whistler's portrait of Comte de Montesquiou, a harlequin of letters, there was no actual harlequinade on the part of the painter, though he may have seemed indulgent to it in his model. How much less is there in the Sarasate, where a genuine artist, but not a profound artist, is seen making his astonishing appearance, violin in hand, out of darkness upon a stage where he is to be the virtuoso. Sarasate's tone is a miracle, like Melba's, and he added to this miracle of technique a Southern fire, which used to go electrically through his audience. He has his temperament and his technique, nothing else.

The man who holds the violin in his hands is a child, pleased to please; not a student or a diviner. And Whistler has rendered all this, as truthfully as Watts has rendered the very different problem of Joachim, in perhaps the greatest of his portraits. Joachim is in the act of playing; he bends his brows over the music which he is studying, not reading; if there is any platform or any audience, he is unconscious of them; he is conscious only of Beethoven. Note how Sarasate handles the violin. It is a child, a jewel. He is already thinking of the sound, the flawless tone, not of Beethoven, though he may be just going to play the Kreutzer Sonata. Whistler has caught him, poised him, posed him, another butterfly and alive. Imagine Sarasate painted by Watts, or indeed in any way but Whistler's. There might have been other great pictures, but no other such interpretation.

And so, in this little dancer, who skips out of time into eternity, more ghostly than flesh and blood, more real than a dream; this image and symbol of wavering, unripe things, "sweet, not lasting," a toy, a perfume; we have another interpretation, not less subtle than that of the childlike and worldly musician, an interpretation of the dancing-girl, which renders for our own age something of what the Greeks rendered on vases and in marble reliefs for theirs. For our sophisticated age that he may give its essence, he gives us the last sophistication; a girl travestied as a boy, and scarcely a girl, but a child and a dance which mimics the games of childhood. The clothes of the dancer are almost of the same colour as the background, dull gold; only the incredibly thin legs dance out of the shadow, in tights of pale gold; and there is a spot of red in each hand, in the handles of the skipping-rope. The face, with its eyes like violets, looks out with calmness that is a little old and a little weary; it is the child playing for other people's pleasure. As I think of the picture the attitude comes back to me almost like that of one condemned to gaiety and perpetual motion, with something of cruelty in the insistence of its light step. I have no doubt that the impression comes from that ambiguous air which Whistler gives to so many of his people; a mystery which was part of his art, of his way of painting, as much as of his vision or intention.

Now look from this ghostly dancer to the solid woman who sits, so piercingly alive, in her white dress and with her knot of black curls, Goya's *Duchess of Alva*. Here is a living person, not evoked out of nothing, and left to waver between two lights, but a strong, actual and passionate woman of flesh and blood, thought out by the painter before he began to see her on his canvas, mastered, and then built up in a close copy of nature. It is queer, forbidding, not instantly interesting even; reality not twisted into anything grim and fantastic, as in the wonderful miniatures on ivory which are to be seen in the same gallery. It is Goya creating in rivalry with nature, resolute not to go beyond nature's pattern. And, if you care to see how far skill of imitation can go, not a creation but a copy, look at the two *Dutch Babies* of Cornelius de Vos beside it; a piece of homely comedy, an exact record of that comedy of nature which seems almost to force humour upon its copyist. What attentiveness, in the painter, to every fold and pucker in the flesh, and to the unconscious solemnity of the staring eyes! We see the Dutchman's tenacious, friendly, and dispassionate observation; and how strangely it contrasts with the Spaniard's eager heat and the nervous sensitiveness of the American.

THE NEW GALLERY AND
OTHERS

GOING into the New Gallery one seems to find oneself in a brilliant shop, its shelves and cases stocked with bric-à-brac; and it is only gradually that one distinguishes, among the many pieces of sculpture around the central hall, the few serious ones. Jacques Blanche has dazzled but not greatly interested us by his blue silks; and there are gowns and faces which may be Sargent's or Shannon's, or (who knows?) neither's, but that is for the catalogue and scarcely for our eyes to decide. Then there is the "Sargent presentation portrait," a soldier with a grand head, standing in dazzling white undress uniform by the side of a toppling pageant, symbolic of its kind, with crimson-and-gilt properties, a white helmet, and soaring up and from a heaped table, a big Imperial globe. The thing is spectacular, rhetorical, like the sculpture or architecture of Bernini; but it is the one big masterly piece of work in the exhibition. For chic and amusing characterisation, nothing comes up to Jacques Blanche's portrait of Mme. Colette Willy, which seems to give one the whole woman, so feminine, so witty, and so Parisian, with a subdued indication of the two persons of her duologues, Tony-Chien and Kiki-la-Doucette, seated gravely at her feet.

At Mr. Paterson's Gallery one is sure of finding only a few things and those things good. But in the exhibition of etchings there is something to be seen besides the fine collection of Rembrandts, Méryons, Manets, Keanes and Whistlers. There is a small and exquisite bronze by

Barye, almost or wholly unknown, a lioness; and as one walks round the room to look at the etchings one's eyes return continually to the sleek, delicate, and formidable beast on the table. Among the etchings, those by Manet are the chief novelty; the Méryons, though unusually fine impressions, are mostly familiar; there are some very beautiful Charles Keanes, *The Canal Lock*, for instance, and the *Art Student*.

To compare Manet and Whistler is to see two worlds of sight, and it is possible to pass from the one to the other without more than a personal preference; they are on an equality. Each reveals himself in his etchings, not less distinctly than in his pictures, though Whistler's etchings extend over thirty years, while Manet's were done for the most part between 1860 and 1866. In the work of Manet his etchings are almost an accident, while in Whistler's they are an essential part of the work. But in these thirty etchings, only six of which are on the walls, and the others are to be seen in a portfolio, one sees the real, the characteristic Manet, his simplicity of sight, over against Whistler's subtlety; his hard outline, his sense of form, over against the colour and wavering outline of Whistler. Look at the *Olympia* almost as fine as the picture itself, with its strong grip on darkness; the *Three Cats*, placed with astonishing decision, each in its place; the *Berthe Morisot*, a masterpiece of character-drawing, and the *Eva Gonzales*, a miracle of suggested form and character, in mere big scrawl of outline. Perhaps the most delightful as a picture is *La Queue à la Boucherie*, done in 1871, and certainly nothing is more brilliant in its dexterity than the last of all, the *Jeanne*

53

of 1882. Occasionally, as in *L'Acteur tragique*, we feel a kind of rhetoric in the emphasis; as we feel, very disagreeably, and for a reason, in the head of Poe. Compare this conventional portrait, done after a photograph, with the startling Baudelaire and the splendid Banville done from life; and you will see what happens when Manet has not the model under his eye. There is a *Marine*, a fantastic ship on a fantastic sea, which is just such another attempt to put something invented and imaginary in the place of a real thing ardently seen. For the most part these are studies of Spanish dancers and Spanish actors, people who helped Manet to realise Spain before he went there, but when he was already under the influence of Spanish painting. They have the sombre elegance, poise and pungency of Spanish people; and Manet and Baudelaire have had each an equal share in immortalising that dancer, Lola de Valence, whom Manet's etching shows us, all nervous energy and arrested movement, while, in Baudelaire's stanza,

> *On voit scintiller en Lola de Valence*
> *Le charme inattendu d'un bijou rose et noir.*

And there are pictures of old men smoking, of a boy blowing bubbles, of a kneeling youth drinking out of a gourd (one of the best), and a *Toilette* which may have led the way to Degas. In all these the beauty is a form of energy, and comes out of the fresh unflinching way in which a very ordinary thing is seen and captured. It is singular to remember that there was a time not so many years ago, when Manet was looked upon as wildly eccentric; he seems to us now so simple, so straightforward, so obvious almost in his aim at truth. What Whistler aims at is an aspect much more cunningly chosen, a rarity of aspect, in which the things may be caught off-guard, and set, dainty and unexpected, before one. In his real and rare world, indicated well enough by these fifteen etchings of many periods, there is only one failure to achieve exactly what he had meant to do, the exact shade of beauty; the St. James's Street, which means for Whistler very little. But in these examples of Venice, Dutch and French sets, in the Thames etchings, and in the portraits, we see the Whistler who was one of the lyric poets of sight. Only Rembrandt, among etchers, was a greater poet; and even Rembrandt was only greater in the sense in which Milton is greater than Crashaw. At the Leicester Galleries there is a collection of thirteen drawings by Helleu, and it is amusing and instructive to go from the severe and serious company at Mr. Paterson's to the rather bad company which awaits us there. At the Painter-Etchers' there were some portrait-heads in which Helleu was seen as hardly more than a fashion-plate artist, prettifying fashionable women with all the same skill of his superficial draughtsmanship. His drawings are at least far more alive; they give us chic in all its hasty expressiveness, a wholly Parisian art, hardly more serious than agile journalism, but how clever of its kind! There are snatches, snapshots, heads and hands caught at unguarded moments, a pouncing skill in catching the likeness, the movement. Here are little girls, young women, sprawling on floors and sofas, leaning out of balconies, reading newspapers aslant in armchairs; and they are there, casual as in life. The skill of hand fails altogether when it attempts a mother and child, as in No. 10; and is at its best when it suggests, as in the girl on the sofa, the animal at watch or at rest.

ROMANCE, REALITY AND
IMAGINATION

A PICTURE which has never been left quite alone for nearly fifty years has at last been finished, and Holman Hunt's long since famous *Lady of Shalott* stands in a room by itself at Messrs. Tooth's Galleries. It has been achieved with almost no sign of age, and the painter is now seventy-seven. It is, indeed, like a survival from the past, for the whole sentiment of the picture is the sentiment of the poem of Tennyson which it illustrates, and how remote that seems from us already! In the poem of Tennyson and in the picture of Holman Hunt I find the same qualities: no imagination, no reality, but a lovely fancy, a coloured and delectable romance. Romance, properly speaking, is not a real thing nor a thing seen in vision, and thus can have the truth of neither real nor imaginative existence: it is a compromise, made for pleasure; a kind of game, in which everything is much comelier and more engaging than things are in the world, and yet only picked out after the world's patterns. The poem of Tennyson is like a lovely toy, and one listens to it with a child's pleasure. And the picture is a toy also, a solemn toy for grown-up people, and Hunt has explained it as an allegory and we are free to see as much or as little meaning in it as we like. The meaning which he is at so much pains to prove in his prose is of little consequence; what matters is the atmosphere of romance, the romantic details; the circles of frame, mirror, panels and web, the soft bright threads of the web, the Rapunzel hair, the

57

peacock bodice, the tapestry on the walls, the carpet on the floor. Romance is in all the lines and colours, knotted in the threads of the web and wound into the listless hurricane of hair through which the red gold of the frame of the mirror shows like red roses tangled. In the smooth unmodelled face there is beauty of a kind which we shall not find in the smooth faces painted by painters who do not dream. The dream is not wholly rendered by painting, it is separate from it, but it shows through the painting. You know that the painter has dreamed, and the face comes to you with his message. And, in judging the picture, in which there is so much colour that is beautiful and so much colour that is false, in which detail sometimes tells against detail, and in which the design itself (that cartoon which has waited fifty years to be achieved in paint) is finer than the finished picture, we must remember that this is not a real room with a landscape reflected in a real mirror, but a room as unreal as the reflections in that mirror, a room itself seen in the mirror of the painter's brain. It is no actual sunlight which reddens the finger-tips of the lady as she turns from the mirror to the window which looks out on a Camelot of dreams. She and her web and the window are all fancies, symbols of romance; they are reflection within reflection, dream within dream. It belongs to the period of Tennyson and of the early William Morris, a period which is now remote enough to have become history. That period has its importance in the development of our poetry and of our painting, and in Holman Hunt's picture I seem to see it concentrated. It is a picture that would find its proper place in the Tate Gallery. The Chantrey Trust, as we know, is content with an imitation Pre-Raphaelite under the same roof, honourably outside the official collection.

A selection from the pictures of Staats Forbes has been on view for some time in the Grafton Galleries; and, in spite of a certain amount of mediocre or dubious work, how well that collection stands out from many official collections! There is the finest Rousseau I have ever seen, a vigorous Daumier, some lovely Millet drawings (together with a version of the *Angelus* which suggests the coloured postcard) one or two fine Monticellis and early Corots, and at least one fine Fantin-Latour, a very interesting Courbet (*The Silent Pool*) and one good Diaz (*Cloud Effect*) among a dozen or two of bad ones; with modern Dutchmen, the Marises, Mauve and others, at their best. The modern Dutchmen are to be seen everywhere just now; it is significant, for in them we get perhaps the finest kind of reality which we are capable of understanding. There has indeed been an exhibition only now closed; of an English painter who has his own way of seeing things, but I doubt if Tonks's pictures at the Carfax Gallery have drawn very many visitors. There were sanguines of an admirable energy (in which one recognised the origin of some of the most powerful draughtsmanship of the younger men) and water-colours in which a personal vision was expressed with the sharp and sudden lack of skill. Here was a man who is content to go straight for the essential part of his design, the essential note of his colour, and to leave the rest alone. But to see the average work which average people find it easy to like, we have only to go to the Leicester Galleries, and there we will

59

find the trivial pretty pictures of Boughton, of which the best that we can say is that the prettiness is an honest prettiness.

Thus it is to the modern Dutchmen that we must go if we want reality seen by painters, not as illustrations and not in terms of pretty unreality. Israels paints rather deliberately for the gallery, but Mauve and the Marises and Weissenbruch paint "Nature seen through a temperament," and they appeal to us so much because we have no difficulty in putting ourselves in their place, and in seeing through their eyes. At Mr. Patterson's Gallery there are some pictures by a Dutchman who lives in England and paints English landscapes in the Dutch manner. There is capacity in Mr. Bruckman's work, and it is interesting to see how Dutch England can become when it is seen honestly through selecting Dutch eyes: the mudflats at Rye, warehouses on the Thames, even Whitechapel, after a little arranging! England indeed seems to bring out Mr. Bruckman's best qualities, for there is not nearly so much feeling, or so successful a method, in the large picture of the North *Amsterdam*. At the Dutch Gallery, besides the usual Dutch pictures, good of their kind, there is a vigorous little painting by Barge—a tree tossing its branches against a stormy sky—which stands out from among them in a personal way of its own; and there are drawings of Legros and C. H. Shannon, and one of Shannon's pictures, from the Forbes collection, which is as suave in rhythm, as delicate in colour, as gracious and gentle as anything he has ever done. But the one great picture is hung outside the door on the landing of the staircase; the sketch of Daumier for his *Christ*

Mocked. It is a sketch, a shadow, but all is there; all the world in the scrawled heads and faces, and the devil perhaps in the finger of theworld's scorn pointed at the Christ, a ghost of judgment, who stands and is patient. Here, in this cartoon, is great imaginative work; and to compare it with Holman Hunt's marvellously finished picture is to realise something of the gulf which divides imagination (that is, spiritual reality) from fancy (that is the game of romance).

GORDON CRAIG AND THE
PAINTERS IN
TEMPERA

THE twenty-six designs for stage scenes and costumes which Gordon Craig is showing at the Bruton Galleries contain the best work which he has yet done. They are not meant to be taken merely as drawings, but rather as drawings for theatrical decorations; but some of them, taken merely as drawings, have a fine pictorial quality. No. 23, a stage scene for Herr von Hoffmansthal's adaptation of *Venice Preserved*, suggests certainly a good stage grouping, but it has qualities of design and colour which make it subtly decorative in itself. And the drawing next to it, the street scene with arcades, how pictorial that is also! But in addition to this almost accidental merit which some have, all have an extraordinary merit as suggestions for stage pictures. Everywhere a wild and exquisite scenic imagination builds up shadowy structures which seem to have arisen by some strange hazard, and to the sound of an unfamiliar music, and which are often literally like music in the cadences of their design. All have dignity, remoteness, vastness; a sense of mystery, an actual emotion in their lines and faint colours. There is poetry in this bare prose framework of stage properties, a quality of grace which is almost evasive, and seems to point out new possibilities of drama, as it provides new, scarcely hoped for, possibilities to the dramatist.

Take, for instance, *The Masque of London*. It is Piranesi, and it is London of to-day, seen in lineal vision, and it is a design, not merely on paper, but built up definitely between the wings of the stage. It is a vast scaffolding, rising out of ruins, and ascending to toppling heights; all its crazy shapes seem to lean over in the air, and at intervals a little weary being climbs with obscure patience. In No. 4 we see the room in the castle at Elsinore into which Ophelia is to come with her bewildered singing; and the room waits, tall, vague, prepared for beauty and madness. There is another room in No. 15, with tall doors and windows and abrupt pools of light on the floor; and another in No. 24 with its significant shadows, in two enigmatic figures, in which a drama of Maeterlinck might find its own atmosphere awaiting it. And in No. 25 all is gesture; walls, half-opened doors, half-seen windows, the huddled people at a doorway, and the doorway, and the tall figure of a woman raised up in the foreground who seems to motion to them vehemently. Colour co-operates with line in effects of rich and yet delicate vagueness; there are always the long, straight lines, the sense of height and space, the bare surfaces, the subtle, significant shadows out of which Craig has long since learned to evoke stage pictures more beautiful and more suggestive than any that have been seen on the stage in our time. The whole stage art of Craig is a protest against realism, and it is to realism that we owe whatever is most conspicuously bad in the mounting of plays at the present day. Wagner did some of the harm; for he refused to realise some of the necessary limitations of stage illusion, and persisted in believing that the stage artist could compete successfully with nature in the production of landscape, light and shadow. Yet Wagner himself protested against the heaps of unrealising detail under which Shakespeare was buried, in his own time, on the German stage, as he is buried on the English stage in our own. No scene-painter, no scene shifter, no limelight man will ever delude us by his moon or meadow or moving clouds of water. His business is to aid the poet's illusion, that illusion of beauty which is the chief excuse for stage plays at all, when once we have passed beyond the "rose-pink and dirty drab," in Meredith's sufficing phrase, of stage romance and stage reality. The distinction, the incomparable merit of Craig is that he conceives his setting as the poet conceives his drama. The verse in most Shakespearean revivals rebounds from backcloth of metallic solidity; the scenery shuts in the players, not upon Shakespeare's dream, but upon as nearly as possible "real" historical bric-à-brac. What Craig does, or would do if he were allowed to do it, is to open all sorts of magic casements and to thrust back all kinds of real and probable limits, and to give, at last, a little scope for the imagination of the playwright who is also a poet.

BOOKS, BINDINGS AND
A TITIAN

NOTHING in London is more difficult than to get books well bound and at the same time cheaply bound. This is why I am glad to see that Douglas Cockerell is having an exhibition of his bindings at the Booklovers' Library in Hanover Square. Specimens are to be seen of very costly and elaborate bindings, and I do not care for all the intricacies of inlay and all the flourishes of gold which decorate them. Some indeed are quite simple and admirable. But what especially interests me is to find here a binding in half sealskin or sheepskin, plainly done, with a few good straight lines in gold and no further ornament. The work seems to be well and strongly done, the leather is guaranteed to be free from mineral acid, and the colours that I have seen are well chosen and well combined with the colours of the paper sides and end papers. I have not seen any bindings on sale in London that seem to me so adequate for all ordinary purposes. Books bound in the cheapest of these bindings would look well in any library and would always be good to handle. They have none of the tricks, mechanical patterns, foolish or fantastic lettering of almost all books bound cheaply to order.

In most countries, except England and America, books are issued in paper covers, almost all of a piece, without the slightest attempt to individualise or to beautify them. The rag of primrose-coloured or other paper which carries the title, duplicated from the title-page inside, is meant to do no more than hold the sheets together until they are put into the binder's hands. Books are thus issued cheaply, and can be bound according to one's means or taste. I think the plan is a better plan than the English plan of putting a common cloth binding on every book which, as a rule, one neither likes nor takes the trouble to replace. Very little money can be spent by the publisher on the binding of his ordinary books, and whatever money he does spend is generally worse than wasted. Some publishers are indeed beginning to see that a cloth-bound book gains by every inch of design that you omit from it. But, as a rule, the cheaper the book the gaudier and the more abominable the decoration. I am assured that the glitter of gold on a cover draws the eye of the purchaser with an irresistible attraction. If so, I would cheerfully do without a reader so vulgarly allured. I do not say that a book may not be elaborately ornamented and yet be a beautiful book. The binding by Althea Gyles of Yeats' *Wind Among the Reeds*, not only in the white and gold vellum, but in the blue and gold cloth, is a beautiful binding, full of an ardent lineal imagination. Ricketts' cover for *Silverpoints* is a beautiful piece of fancy, subtly decorative. And the cover which Rossetti designed for his own poems has at once severity and splendour, and completes the art of the poems. But how rarely do we find such successes as these, even among the work of good decorators, and how hopeless it is to look for even moderately good decoration in the conventional or incoherent designs turned out by binders' hacks, and plastered upon the covers of books for purely commercial reasons! There is not a publisher in London who can be trusted to put a square inch of decoration on the cover of a book without making the book unsightly. Safety is to be found only in plain lettering, as few publishers can be quite relied upon to keep their plain lettering really plain and really uniform. We have good printers; we have, in the printers of the Chiswick Press especially, printers of taste; yet it is hardly less difficult to get a book satisfactorily printed than to get it satisfactorily bound. A publisher here and there is beginning to realise that to use two kinds of type on the same page is not to ornament that page; that to space out letters, words and lines is fatal to the look of a page of print, as form and colour; and that to be stingy or capricious in the matter of margins is to abandon all chance of making a page look well. Few are willing to sacrifice the utility of a headline to the comeliness of its absence; hardly more are satisfied to let a title-page be the briefest and closest statement of the case, and no more. For the most part all this is the fault of the publishers, not of the printers, who are generally willing to adopt a rational suggestion. But publishers have their fixed ideas of propriety, and can rarely be persuaded to wholly abandon them. At the most they make compromises, and all compromises are fatal. The only book that I have been able to bring out entirely according to my own ideas is the two-volume edition of my poems published by Heinemann, and even in this, a single, tiny, yet to me important detail was rearranged by the printer's reader after I had passed every page for press. As far as I can judge, most writers are quite indifferent to the form in which their works appear. I do not understand this indifference any more than I understand a painter who

puts his picture into a frame of any pattern, so long as
the frame fits the size of his canvas. But, as books become cheaper and cheaper, and competition cries louder
and louder, it is more and more difficult to bring about
this so desirable harmony between the inner meaning
and the outer form of a book.

The most beautiful books of our time are of course
those of William Morris, and next to them I would put
the Vale Press publications of Ricketts, which indeed I
can read for myself with greater pleasure. A much simpler
attempt to produce beautiful books quite undecorated
but printed in a fine, simple eighteenth-century type on
paper made of linen rags and without bleaching chem-
icals, has been made in Ireland by Miss E. C. Yeats, at
the Dun-Emer Press, Dundrum, County Dublin. Only
fine books have as yet been printed and, of necessity, in
very small editions; for the whole work is done on a hand
press by Miss Yeats and by two young girls, her assistants.
The type was selected and the first instruction given by
Emery Walker; each book is simpler, more harmonious,
more satisfactory, than the last, and W. B. Yeats' *Stories
of Red Hanrahan* seems to me to give us the fine homely
imagination of the stories (a re-casting in choicer and
more peasant-like speech of a part of *The Secret Rose*)
precisely as that work should come to us, the frame com-
pleting the picture.

But all this time I have been speaking of pictures only
metaphorically, and there is a picture to be seen in London which should be seen by everyone who cares for pictures, a Titian, a great Titian, the Aretino of the Palazzo
Chigi, now on view at Messrs. Colnaghi's in Pall Mall.

As a picture, as a piece of painting, I am not sure that it is so fine as the Aretino of the Pitti; but as a portrait, as a dramatic study of character, it is finer. It was evidently painted earlier than the other, and is very likely the "sketch" which Aretino did not find pompous and formal enough. The *flagellum principium* lent himself, certainly, with splendid frankness to what was most revealing in the brush of the painter in whom he was proud to proclaim *la consanguinità dell' amicitia*. It is a portrait of a scoundrel and of a man of genius, and both are there in the fraudulent eyes, insolent lips, beaked nose and strong head. He is set down there, without kindness and without malice, to last for eternity, an image of evil power. The painting is severe, sufficient, bare of display, nothing draws off the attention of the eyes from what is meant to arrest and keep them, the head; as in the Darnley Titian, the sumptuous sleeve takes the eyes on their way to the grave face, and brings them back again when the face is done with. Beside this portrait almost every other portrait seems an arrangement or an evasion; here there is nothing but truth, and that vital beauty which grows almost unconsciously out of truth. It is one of the portraits of the world, and I cannot imagine anyone going to see any other while this is in London. That is, if it is ever to leave London.

THE PSYCHOLOGY OF
WATTS

IN a book on Watts which was published nearly two years ago, a popular preacher, setting down Watts as himself neither more nor less than a popular preacher, whose sermons took the form of pictures, assured us, as if on the painter's own authority,"Critics who approach his work from the side of technical excellence do not interest him at all. His endeavour has been to make his pictures as good as works of art as was possible to him, for fear that they should fail altogether in their appeal, but beyond that, their excellence as mere pictures is nothing to him." Now it is quite possible that Watts may have really said or written something of the kind, he may even, when he set himself down to think, have thought it. The conscious mental processes of an artist have often little enough relation with his work as art; by no means every artist is a critic as well as an artist. But to take a great painter at his word, if he assures you that the excellence of his pictures "as mere pictures" is nothing to him; to seriously suppose that at the root of his painting was not the desire to paint; to believe for a moment that great pictorial work has ever been done except by those who were painters first, and everything else afterwards, is to confuse the elementary notions of things, hopelessly and finally. The wild praise of Watts has done as much harm as the wrong praise of Browning. How many people have been led by books to believe that Browning is a great philosophic poet,which he is not;without ever being told that he is a great love-poet, a great lyrical poet!

And so, when we are told that the technical excellence
of Watts's pictures is of little consequence, we can but
answer that to the "painter of earnest truths," as to
all painters, nothing can be of more consequence, for
it is only through this technical excellence that *Hope* or
The Happy Warrior or *Love and Life*, is to be preferred
to the picture leaflet which the district missionary dis-
tributes on his way through the streets. In the penetrating and sympathetic book of Reminiscences by Mrs.
Russell Barrington, an intimate friend and neighbour of
Watts for nearly thirty years, there is indeed no lack of
information about those "aims" which meant so much
to the painter, together with the profoundest respect for
them, but what gives its main value to this page of "con-
temporary history," as the writer justly calls it, is her
real artistic understanding of the whole texture of an
artist's consciousness. She helps us to see how Watts did
what he did by showing us how he was what he was. What
she has done is to give us a psychological study, done with
equal sympathy and acuteness, of a personality which
few people can have had closer opportunities of observ-
ing. Her book is personal in the best and frankest sense.
She has not even the affectation of trying to keep herself
in the background. She tells us quite simply about her
painting and her writing, and how Watts said one of her
drawings was like a Holbein, and how he said that it was
she and not he who had genius; she tells us all this not
for its relation to herself but for its relation to the moods
and views of Watts, his kind and quaint enthusiasms,
his somewhat self-conscious depreciations of self. And instead of leaving us with the impression that she is making

the most of her acquaintance with a great man, we close
the book with the thought: how fortunate was the great
man in having so helpful and so wise a friend.

In these notes, written out of an affectionate but open-
eyed reverence, there are many significant things said
in passing, in which we may find perhaps a deeper truth
than the writer was conscious of. Take these sentences,
for instance:—

"Alone, before his easel, he was consistent—the lofty
thinker, the sensitive seer, the sincere workman. Outside that door he was content to have things vague, unthought out. He did not always care for a spade to be
called a spade. Focalising light on bare facts would at
times 'disturb impressions.' At such times, bare naked
truth was not always what he cared to face—too much
explicitness disturbed and put things out of tune with
the imaginative pictures he had made of a situation."

Is not this glimpse into Watts's mind really a criticism
of his art as well? That readiness to "leave things vague,
unthought out" was a condition of his mind not only outside the studio door but inside it. In how many of his
pictures did not nature "put him out" in a way how different from Whistler's! His imagination was too often
"moving about in worlds not realised," painting noble
emotions, but emotions not visualised with precision.

One of the most significant passages in this book is the
passage in which Watts is described as saying that he
thought he ought to have been a musician instead of a
painter. He heard melodies and harmonies without conscious thought, whereas only one picture had ever come
to him as a vision. He had "revelations in sound," and

said "how strange it was that he never saw a picture as a picture even while in process of painting." He used to speak of his imaginative pictures as "anthems," and there are certainly many of his pictures which exist only through the lyrical qualities of their paint. Can this be said even of the most extraordinary experiments of Turner, where "colour seems to go mad and to speak with tongues"? It seems to me that Turner is never vague, that he is always trying to get closer and closer to something which he really sees. There are times when Watts sees nothing but his noble emotion. He took great interest in the working of his own mind, and would become so much engrossed in the idea which stimulated the painting of his subjects, that the design would probably become a minor consideration. Yet he was fully conscious of the fact that the purpose of a picture can be rendered only through the quality of its design. The painter's business is first and foremost to paint, and no one was ever more conscious of this truism than Watts—feeling that to a true artist, right expression is the inevitable sequel of a fine idea— that they are inseparable.

Many of the most interesting pages of this book are filled with technical details, theories of "flattened curves" in line, theories of pigment of material, which came through hard work, luck and the power of interpreting and thus capturing the meaning of a happy accident. Yet this great artist could not bring himself to see that there is no beauty for the artist so genuine and so enduring as that beauty which is founded on nature. His distaste for working from models was great as a rule. They could help him but little in the chief aims of his work, and their presence in his studio disturbed the solitude which conduced, he thought, to the best development of his ideas.

Just before reading Mrs. Barrington's book I was reading an article in *La Renaissance Latine* by Camille Mauclar, called *Notes sur la Technique et le Symbolisme de Rodin*. Here I find a greater than Watts saying, "Une chose ne peut être belle que si elle est vraie," and again, "La beauté n'est pas un point de départ, mais d'arriv ée."

With an admiration for Greek sculpture not less than that of Watts, we find Rodin saying: "L'Antique, c'est la vie même. Les anciens ont été les plus grands, les plus sérieux, les plus admirables observateur de la nature qu'il y ait jamais eu." And he says further: "Etudier mal l'Antique est pire que l'ignorer; il n'est pas l'alphabet de l'artiste, mais la récompense de son travail." Was there not in much of Watts's work, in much indeed of his aim, a combination of elements out of what had already been done by the greatest artists, rather than out of nature, out of life itself? Is there not a certain limitation in work which already looks so much like what we call an Old Master? In frankly adopting Titian's method as recorded by Boschini, was he not trying to make his work as like Titian's as he could? And is there, in Watts's work, considered as painting, anything in the technique not already implicit in the later work of Titian, in the *Christ Crowned with Thorns*, for instance, at Munich?

PORTRAIT PAINTERS AND
A VELASQUEZ

THERE are more than two hundred portraits at the New Gallery, and about five-and-twenty of them are really interesting; some of the five-and-twenty are really fine. The remainder are either dully capable, or capably conventional, or good and not interesting, or interesting and not good. In one whole room, the North, there are forty-two pictures, of which two have a certain interest, one at least individual; while the others might as well not have been there, for all the impressions they leave on one's memory. And we might go through the other rooms, weeding out portrait after portrait, until a tiny collection remained, among which we might spend an hour, and be tempted to return for other hours on other days.

Having then, made our selection for ourselves, let us look at a few of the really good or interesting things in the gallery. For my part I went back oftenest to two very small pictures in the West room: Millet's portrait of his second wife, and Carrière's portrait of his son. Each is a masterpiece of its kind, and it is possible almost to hesitate between the solid and joyous energy of the one, and the subtle and caressing energy of the other. There is another Millet in another room, a portrait of his first wife, and there are some fine drawings, portraits of painters, Diaz, Rousseau and others; but how frank, easy, engaging, is this picture of the second wife, and what a nicely homely person! Carrière is not as well known here as he should be; in France he is gradually taking a position

among painters similar to Rodin's position among sculptors; and the two together represent all that is finest,
most personal, most profound, in the art of our time.
In this baby's head you will find the most sensitively and
the most tenderly human work in the exhibition; and you
have only to look from it to the many able and adequate
presentments of well-dressed ladies and gentlemen on all
sides, to see the difference between clever painters and
a painter of genius.

On the opposite wall there is a little Whistler, a girl's
head, *Brun et Or*, which you might almost pass without
seeing it but which, once seen, holds the whole of the
mind, in an uneasy speculation.The eyes retain a secret,
though the head and hair may seem to have been painted
only for the colour and dim pattern which they make on
the canvas. A Charles Shannon, near by, a *Lady in a
Black Jacket* says nothing, has nothing to say or retain;
but she exists there in quiet, a silent harmony. On the
next wall there is a Besnard, a man with fierce mous-
taches and frockcoat like a blown mantle, who seems to
have been snatched and flung there, as by a whirlwind.
He lives with angry vitality, while a woman, painted by
Besnard on the wall at the other end of the room, exists
merely to be flesh in sunlight, and Parisian. Harry Mel-
ville painted by Jacques Blanche twists his head and
sucks in his cheeks with a whimsical turn of the whole
body, like one telling a story of acid humour; and one
sees as living a being as the Madame Marchesi of Signor
Mancini who seems actually to move, gesticulate, burst
into speech as if uneasy, and unimprisoned in her frame.
Not far from her, beyond the Orchardson portrait, which

expresses as much of temperament through so personal an autumn colouring, are Corot's portraits of his father and mother, which live with a profound quietude and simplicity of life. In another room we see Daubigny's picture of Corot painting, and the small dainty picture has humour and psychology; an amusing study from life and an interpretation.

Here, then, is a picture one could live with; think of living with any of the two hundred restless modern people on the walls, who are themselves either nervous, or ill, or staring, or attitudinising or content to be dressed fashionably; all except here and there a Whistler or a Carrière or a Charles Shannon. For the most part clothes dominate character; and, if there is character, there is no temperament. The modern multiplying of portraits, made as lifelike as the painter can make them, and, as far as the men are concerned, in uncomely clothes, is a distressing fact. Now everyone who has money can have his portrait, as large as life, thrust on the view of the public in a yearly exhibition, or added to the permanent misery of the world in a private house or public institution. Painters are no longer choosers, in any complete sense, at least they have never been the chosen of so casual a multitude. And there was a time when the narrow round of a medallion was wide enough for the ambition of a conqueror in war. Now the conqueror in business must have his gilt frame, and the conqueror in Parliament his marble bust.

I had written as far as this when I was called into the town, and passing through Bond Street saw an announcement outside Messrs. Agnew's gallery which put all thoughts of modern sculptors or modern portrait painters out of my head. One of the great pictures of the world was on view there, and for sale, the *Venus and Cupid* of Velasquez, formerly at Rokeby Park, the only nude portrait of a woman ever painted by Velasquez. I have gone back to see it twice, and now I know what till now I had only taken on trust, that it is one of the great pictures of the world. The technique is not that of Velasquez' latest and, for the most part, finest period; that excess of delight in the paint itself is as if restrained, confined within the severest limits; the beauty (which is one with truth) of the picture is everything. How precisely Keats had defined what is ultimate in art when he said "Beauty is Truth, Truth Beauty." In this picture there is no mere marriage or happy union of truth and beauty, but a transubstantiation. The woman who lies there on the canvas is the divine animal; the flesh, which is merely flesh, and untouched by the desecration of the ideal, is as innocent and as mysterious as life. She has thrown herself down carelessly; there is no pose, no arrangement; nothing that is in nature is lost, yet something has come into nature, which is, I suppose, imagination, so that this real thing is not a copy but a vision. If this masterpiece, having come to London, should ever leave London, and not take its rightful place in the National Gallery, well, no one will be surprised, but it will be a national shame. Can nothing be done to secure it? There never was a greater painter than Velasquez and we are poor in his work. The possession of this picture would make us rich in his work, among all the galleries of Europe. Does the State care nothing for such national riches? Do Englishmen care nothing? It is now in the National Gallery.

ENGLISH MASTERS AT THE
ROYAL ACADEMY

THE Winter Exhibition at the Royal Academy is profoundly interesting and, but for a few exceptions for which we can only be grateful, it is confined to the work of English artists, from Hogarth to Simeon Solomon. Among the exceptions are such foreign masterpieces as Frans Hals' portrait of himself and his family, a vast canvas which, for vital energy and grasp on life, dominates the whole exhibition. Hals has done more beautiful, more attractive things, but nothing with more certainty of skill (a skill almost indifferent to itself) and nothing fuller of a critical and self-betraying humour. By its side is a Jordaens, a portrait of the painter's wife; and in this loud animal thing, violently and exasperatingly real, one sees how moderate, how well-tempered, was the realism of Hals. There are Van Dykes, a fine portrait of the wife of Snyders and a large romantic *Saint Sabastian*, painful in the brilliance of its insincerity. Near them is Dobson's portrait of Charles I, so like a Van Dyke, and then we have the foreign and older masters, and begin the eighteenth century in England with Hogarth.

Of Hogarth, whose work in paint is so rarely to be seen, there is a delightful minute conversation-piece (*An Assembly at Wanstead House*), which is like one of his finest engravings; there are two charming and vivid portraits of a boy and of a woman; and there is, besides, put down to his name, a crude and powerful head (No. 7) painted in the way in which one might have imagined him to

79

paint if one did not know quite certainly that he never did so. There is a whole series of admirable Reynoldses, and among them, side by side, such characteristic species of his earlier and later work as the portrait of the Countess of Clanwilliam (1765), and that of Jane, Countess of Harrington (1787). In the latter we see his familiar touch and autumn colouring; but the former, cold, elegant, frigidly delicate, is curiously unlike the rest of his work, and has a real charm of its own. Unusual in subject, full of soft and rich beauty, is the *Venus and Piping Boy*, and of the two portraits of himself one is strangely uneasy and apologetic (No. 5), as if the successful painter were conscious that an obscure painter and poet was to write on the margin of his Discourses: "This man was hired to depress art." There are many lovely Gainsboroughs and none more simple in their charm than the portrait of his two daughters (No. 10). Raeburn is seen well, and Wilson characteristically; Turner in many of his manners, as well as in a very clever reflection of what his manner would have been if seen in a cloudy mirror (No. 56). One big piece of Italian romanticism in the first room (the *Adonis*) shows us a Turner happily little known to us, for all his dash and clever splendour. Then there is a *Classical Composition* of 1814, very stiff and solemn, with a little of the coming light already in it, a somewhat matter-of-fact early sea-piece *The Pilot Boat* and a later *Venice* which begins to become visionary; as well as water-colours so precise and so magical, so miraculous in their rendering of aspects and the moods of aspects that one wonders why any painter should ever try again to paint mist, water or storm.

Among later landscapes, none have so exquisite a quality as the two Boningtons, though there is a good, sombre *Hampstead Heath* of Constable, a fine but too pompous Cecil Lawson, and some interesting pictures by Alfred Hunt, both in oil and water-colour, very personal and sensitive in their rendering of effects. The least interesting room is the fifth, which has many dull things and only a few of fine quality; but the two remaining rooms, the fourth and the water-colour room, are in some ways the most interesting in the exhibition. They are largely given up to the work of a few painters, who form a group apart in the painting of the nineteenth century; and chiefly Rossetti, Burne-Jones, and Simeon Solomon. Apart from these three painters the Academy does not represent the whole early Victorian movement with anything approaching to the comprehensiveness of the recent exhibition in Whitechapel; in spite of Millais' delightful naïvely photographic *Sir Isumbras at the Ford*, and at least one very beautiful early water-colour and a tiny water-colour of Leighton (*Jehu*) which comes upon one with a shock of surprise and delight, for it is vital, imaginative, splendid. There is one of the best of Albert Moore's marble women in pale flesh (*White Hydrangeas*) and, along with a too pretty and facile large composition, a small Pinwell (*The Sisters*) which has a personal and delicate quality of design and colour.

The most interesting Burne-Joneses that have been seen for a long time are the three pictures from the legend of St. George and the Dragon, done in 1865–6 for Birket Foster's dining-room. These are ingeniously inserted between work done ten and thirty years later and the con-

trast between the earlier and later work is curiously instructive. In the early pictures the paint is subdued to
the mood of the painter which makes the picture; in one
of them there is an almost Flemish humour in the company of old heads seen on the level of the Princess's feet;
and in all there is a childlike absorption in the heart and
visible images of the story. Already in *Laus Veneris* the
dreams have gone out of the paint, or something hard
and glassy has come between them. But in these first
pictures we have an early Victorian Carpaccio.

Simeon Solomon, a rival at the start of Burne-Jones,
is seen in these rooms for the first time in a way that
does any sort of justice to him. Here there is almost
nothing but good work, while at the separate exhibition
at the Bailie Gallery there was, along with a few good
things, and many things interesting as steps in progress,
such a multitude of things at once violent and inane, at
once helpless and struggling, that it was impossible to
think seriously of what seemed to be the attempts of a
bad poet to express himself in a medium which he had
not mastered. But at the Academy we see what Solomon
at the beginning of his career really could do: the *Moses*,
Love in Winter, and *Hosanna* of the oils; the *Mystery of
Faith*, and *Greek Priest* of the water-colours. In these,
at his best, there is originality of design and a quality
of colour which seems to possess some queer emotional
significance; they have learnt from Rossetti almost as
definite and personal a thing as Burne-Jones has learnt.
In some of the water-colours we see him in the act of
learning: *And He Shall Give His Angels Charge over Thee* is
imitated with great directness, and with real skill and

feeling. In the larger and slightly later water-colours, like the *Prelude to Bach*, everything that had been concentrated into the single heads or the two figures of a design drifts away like smoke and a vacancy comes visibly in. It is with relief that one finds, in the midst of these chilly emblems, a little Rossetti, not much earlier in date, the *Fazio's Mistress* of 1860, where the real swoon of the lady is a swoon of flesh and blood, and not a shadow fainting before a dream. In Rossetti's pictures, then so sensuous with a mere simple physical sensuousness, it is curious to see the ripe flesh without so much as a dream of the soul (as in *Belcolore* and *Bocca Bacciata*) passing into a body like a heavy and sleepy veil (as in the *Mnemosyne* of 1880) into which the soul has come and become weary.

FRENCH PICTURES AT THE
INTERNATIONAL
EXHIBITION

THERE are two hundred and sixty-four numbers in the catalogue of the new exhibition of the International Society at the New Gallery, and there are surprisingly few of these numbers which have no right to be there. This amount and variety of good work makes it impossible to do justice to the exhibition as a whole in the course of a single article. So I shall confine myself mainly to what seems to me the most important sections, of French pictures, only pointing out that the sculpture is of equal importance with the painting and what is perhaps the finest single thing that Rodin has ever done, *Le Baiser*, is to be seen here, not in a cast but in marble, and also an exquisite detail from the *Gates of Hell*, the *Paolo and Francesca*, and that the work of Constantin Meunier fills a whole wall of the central hall, and can be seen and judged quite fairly from these examples. Among the English pictures, which should be seen first and returned to last, are two by Ricketts, the boldest of any; a picture and a portrait by Shannon, both full of grace and decorative charm; a picture (*The Croquet Players*) by Conder, some of the best portraits that Nicholson has yet done, a spirited portrait by Lavery. There is a quiet Segantini, a mountebank of a Boldini, a Thaulow which is like all the other Thaulows. But indeed there is hardly anything which is not worth looking at, for one reason or another; for even when a picture is not altogether good, it is generally at least characteristic. In some ways the two most significant pictures in the exhibition are a small *Paysage* and a *Nature Morte* of Cezanne. At the present moment Cezanne is the most talked of, the most imitated painter in France. The whole *Salon des Indépendants* of 1905 was described as a vast *Hommage à Cezanne*. Painters who look upon Whistler, upon Fantin-Latour, upon Puvis de Chavannes, as belonging already to the past, unite in accepting Cezanne as already a part of the future. It is Time's revenge, and, like all revenge, excessive. Cezanne has reduced painting to a kind of science, the science of disempassioned technique. "Cezanne," says Charles Morice, "ne s'intéresse pas plus à un visage qu'à une pomme, et celui-la comme celle-ci n'ont d'autre valeur à ses yeux que d'être des 'valeurs', parce que Cezanne n'a que des yeux." The landscape and the still-life study are seen with exactly the same childlike intentness, seen in the child's conversation of hard outline, and with all the emphasis of an eye which chases sentiment out of natural things, that it may take them naked and alone. But, it may be questioned, are things ever naked or alone in nature? Look from Cezanne to Carrière and you will see that everything in the picture, this *Maternité*, this *Mère et Fille*, is made up of correspondences, of the harmonies which envelop and unite life with life, life with nature; that here is a vision of reality so intense that the mere statement of facts no longer needs emphasis. Cezanne's "nature morte" is a lump of the world cut with a knife; in Carrière the rhythm of the mother and child almost evades the limits of the frame, seems a wave of the sea arrested in its motion and as if still in movement. In Carrière,

85

as in Rodin, there are no specimens, but growing things, the flower scarcely plucked, still alive from the root, a part not yet cut off from universal nature. And that is why Rodin leaves the foundations of his figures unshaped in the marble, why he gives the animate being some foothold on the earth; and why Carrière evokes a mist or twilight which clothes his humanity with that tenderness that lurks transformingly behind our eyes when we look on one another, not in observation (which is science) but in love (which is the beginning of art).

And now turn to Manet, who is to be seen in one of the most famous of his later *plein-air* pictures, *Le Linge*, in a small picture of bathers and in one of the greatest of his portrait heads, the head which was one of the masterpieces of the Glasgow Exhibition, and remains perhaps the picture one would most like to possess of anything in the International. George Moore, who has written better about Manet than anyone else, has said with admirable truth: "In Whistler there is an exquisite and inveigling sense of beauty; in Degas there is an extraordinary acute criticism of life; and so the least brutal section of the public ended by pardoning Whistler his brush work and Degas his beautiful drawing. But in Manet there is nothing but good painting." Is not that a hard thing to pardon, because a hard thing to understand? In this head there is a magic which is not magic at all, so far as magic is an evasion or a message from outside nature; the life that is there is a life of frank paint, neither asserting nor concealing itself; there is no sentiment which we can be conscious of, no tenderness as with Carrière; yet still less is there the scientific coldness of Cezanne. It is as if the painter were like the sun itself: an energy beyond good and evil, an immense benevolence, creating without choice or preference out of the need of giving birth to life. There never was such an homage to light, to light as the principle of life, as in *Le Linge*, where the vivifying rays of that impartial sunlight can soak with equal thirst into the ugliness of the child and into the loveliness of the linen. And you may hate the picture as you might hate a day of overpowering heat, yet be no more able to get away from it than you could withdraw from the ardour of nature.

I believe the same thing has been said about Besnard, but for my part I find it harder to realise. There is a huge picture of his here, and several small ones, and they seize the attention, displease it, set it questioning. Here, at least, are no evasions; and with Besnard almost more than with Manet, painting becomes a sort of wager. If he always wins, it is on his own terms; he convinces you only that that is how he sees, not that you could see like him. And he drives straight for his natural effects, with a violent skill of hand, pouring aspect after aspect upon you with a complete power of rendering what his eyes have absorbed. He appears to accept no convention, to go straight to nature; only concentrating his means towards his end, so that each picture bursts upon you with the force of a single attack. Renoir, who has something of the same determination, has nothing like the same concentration, and offers you his wares more indifferently. The three pictures here are all typical. The ball, under the trees of some Vauxhall of the period, is full of savour and gives us the gross gaiety of the scene with gross gaiety.

To think of Manet's picture of the Luxembourg Gardens is to realise all the difference that is made to one's pleasure when things are seen in a distinguished way. The Crowd in Manet's picture is not nearly so much under the sunlight, but it is a scene in a poem of Musset, while Renoir's is an illustration of Zola. Renoir's naked woman is a monstrous doll; one could wish that he had seen her with anger, as Degas sees his shapeless bodies in tubs; but, no, he sees her with satisfaction, he paints her with flattering intentions. In the landscape there is something of the same luxuriant fatness.

There are three pictures here by Degas, the late one not very interesting, but the two early pictures both interesting and unusual. The *Savoisienne* is hardly more than solid, well-defined, minutely executed work; but the *Blanchisseuses*, almost as precise, almost as elaborately finished, has all the surprising movement, the critical observation of the later work; and its beauty will be easier for many people to distinguish. It seems to have been painted just at the moment of transition from what was partly Ingres to what was wholly Degas. In a picture of *Danseuses*, near by, Forain is seen doing no more than an inferior Degas; and in the two dry scenes from the law courts the paint is hardly a help to him; a third picture, *Dans les Coulisses*, suggests more of the witty draughtsman, whose line is so full of malice of the intelligence.